Teaching Children Online

MM Textbooks

Advisory Board:

Professor Colin Baker, *University of Wales, Bangor, UK*

Professor Viv Edwards, *University of Reading, Reading, UK*

Professor Ofelia García, *Columbia University, New York, USA*

Dr Aneta Pavlenko, *Temple University, Philadelphia, USA*

Professor David Singleton, *Trinity College, Dublin, Ireland*

Professor Terrence G. Wiley, *Arizona State University, Tempe, USA*

MM Textbooks bring the subjects covered in our successful range of academic monographs to a student audience. The books in this series explore education and all aspects of language learning and use, as well as other topics of interest to students of these subjects. Written by experts in the field, the books are supervised by a team of world-leading scholars and evaluated by instructors before publication. Each text is student-focused, with suggestions for further reading and study questions leading to a deeper understanding of the subject.

All books in this series are externally peer-reviewed.

Full details of all the books in this series and of all our other publications can be found on http://www.multilingual-matters.com, or by writing to Multilingual Matters, St Nicholas House, 31-34 High Street, Bristol BS1 2AW, UK.

MM Textbooks: 14

Teaching Children Online

A Conversation-based Approach

Carla Meskill and Natasha Anthony

MULTILINGUAL MATTERS
Bristol • Blue Ridge Summit

DOI https://doi.org/10.21832/MESKIL2012

Library of Congress Cataloging in Publication Data
A catalog record for this book is available from the Library of Congress.
Names: Meskill, Carla, author. | Anthony, Natasha, author.
Title: Teaching Children Online: A Conversation-based Approach/
  Carla Meskill and Natasha Anthony.
Description: Bristol, UK; Blue Ridge Summit, PA, USA: Multilingual Matters,
  [2018] | Series: MM Textbooks: 14 | Includes bibliographical references and index.
Identifiers: LCCN 2018028666| ISBN 9781788922012 (hbk : alk. paper) |
  ISBN 9781788922005 (pbk : alk. paper) | ISBN 9781788922043 (kindle)
Subjects: LCSH: Web-based instruction. | Internet in education. |
  Education, Elementary—Computer-assisted instruction. |
  Education, Secondary—Computer-assisted instruction.
Classification: LCC LB1044.87 .M47 2018 | DDC 371.33/44678—dc23
  LC record available at https://lccn.loc.gov/2018028666

British Library Cataloguing in Publication Data
A catalogue entry for this book is available from the British Library.

ISBN-13: 978-1-78892-201-2 (hbk)
ISBN-13: 978-1-78892-200-5 (pbk)

Multilingual Matters
UK: St Nicholas House, 31-34 High Street, Bristol BS1 2AW, UK.
USA: NBN, Blue Ridge Summit, PA, USA.

Website: www.multilingual-matters.com
Twitter: Multi_Ling_Mat
Facebook: https://www.facebook.com/multilingualmatters
Blog: www.channelviewpublications.wordpress.com

The policy of Multilingual Matters/Channel View Publications is to use papers that are natural, renewable and recyclable products, made from wood grown in sustainable forests. In the manufacturing process of our books, and to further support our policy, preference is given to printers that have FSC and PEFC Chain of Custody certification. The FSC and/or PEFC logos will appear on those books where full certification has been granted to the printer concerned.

Typeset by Deanta Global Publishing Services Limited.
Printed and bound in the UK by Short Run Press Ltd.
Printed and bound in the US by Thomson-Shore, Inc.

Contents

Teaching children online: a conversation-based approach

Introduction

We first began thinking about writing this book about 10 years ago when we observed two things going on. First, instructors and instructional designers were trying to fit round pegs into square holes; that is, traditional, live classroom content and instructional processes into online formats. Second, when those round pegs became square, when instructional design threw tradition out of the window and focused on the affordances of the medium that best suited teaching and learning, phenomenally powerful instruction resulted: instruction that was in many ways as effective as traditional means. At the heart of these new ways of conceptualizing what could happen online to affect deep learning was communication. As we know from looking around at popular uses of handheld and desktop devices, it is the social that drives the bulk of our activity with these mediums. People like communicating online both synchronously (in real time) and asynchronously (not determined by time). With communication at the heart of effective teaching and learning, online venues make eminent sense. And so, we had a mission: to spell out for new and experienced online teachers what conversation-based online instruction looks like and how they can make the medium's communication affordances work for them. That is what this book is about.

Purpose of this book

This text presents practical information and illustrations of effective online teaching practices with children in online forums. Its focus is on the rich *instructional conversations* that we can develop and in which we can engage children in order to instruct and enrich through active communication. Whether you teach or plan to teach fully online, in a blended or hybrid format (partially online, partially live), this text will provide a wealth of stimulating guidance in the use of instructional conversations to achieve optimal learning.

There are three main reasons why we wrote this book: first, we both thoroughly enjoy reading, researching, discussing and implementing online instruction. This is in great part due to our shared love of language and our view that the language of instruction is uniquely and powerfully potent in online venues. The second reason is that we see a large gap in material supporting online educators in their work. Our text moves well beyond prescriptive steps and structures that constitute the bulk of 'how to teach online' texts to authentic, concrete illustrations and explications of excellence in action in online teaching. In this way, we give new and practicing online teachers a window into effective instruction and the anatomy by which it is constructed and carried out *conversationally*. As more educators move to online platforms, we feel an urgency to direct them to consider instruction that takes optimal advantage of the many and rich affordances of online *communication* as a means of not duplicating what one does in the classroom. Our third and final reason for this text is that the instructional strategies we present are timeless. They represent optimal forms of instruction regardless of technological advancements in delivery formats.

To us, teaching online is about opportunities and we feel very strongly that with careful consideration of the communicative nature of effective instructional processes educators will not only become more attuned to their craft, but will witness remarkable leaps in the breadth, depth and enthusiasm attendant to their students' learning. We are confident that the illustrations, analyses and discussion we include will lead readers to not only appreciate the powerful conversational possibilities of online teaching, but will take these possibilities to new levels, to new heights in their quest for excellence.

The growth of online instruction across age groups has been exponential. This is for a number of reasons, many of which we discuss in Chapter 1. The place of online learning for children has expanded out of recognition that (1) online instruction can fill curricular gaps experienced by small schools with limited offerings and even large schools whose curriculum may not extend as far as the needs and interests of individual students; (2) online instruction can ensure that children who are otherwise unable to attend school due to physical and psychological reasons can keep up with their peers; and (3) online instruction is growing in appeal and is becoming the instructional mode of choice for many young people. How courses are designed and offered varies a great deal with many large-scale providers employing standardized templates and boilerplate content. This text takes potential and practicing online educators beyond such structures and invites careful consideration of the instructional conversations afforded by the online medium. Throughout, we speak of **online instructional conversations** as they take place in fully online asynchronous/synchronous courses as well as blended courses (courses whereby a part of the instructional time is not online and the other part is).

Audiences

Who is this book written for? This text can complement courses in teacher education across age levels and subject areas. For courses that specifically address online instruction, it can serve as the focal required reading for approaches that value instructional communication as central to the learning enterprise. This text is also ideal for novice and veteran adjuncts or consultants who design and deliver courses for young people online. And, finally, as more businesses employ online instructors as freelancers, this text becomes a valuable source of support and guidance.

This is both a practical guide and a catalyst for deepening one's craft. In each chapter, we discuss a given mode of online communication – an *online venue* – and its affordances. An affordance is a characteristic or potentiality of something to be used for different purposes. The qualities of something that define its purpose: in this case, the instructional possibilities that different online modes carry. We provide illustrations, discussions and direction that the reader can consider adapting and incorporating into his or her work. Our aim is that readers/educators develop instructional conversation expertise in their teaching.

Our philosophy/approach

We have been keenly interested in the theory and practice of **online teaching and learning** since the mid-nineties. This has much to do with our joint scholarship in and passion for language and technology. As a team, we enjoy reading, researching and publishing on the topic and over the years have developed a joint philosophy concerning online instruction: that is, that effective online instruction is *communicative*. How and why we interact with course content and with others about course content take place through speaking and writing. It is within that speaking and writing that learning and development flourish.

Suggestions for readers

This book can be read and used in any number of ways. As a course book in a professional development setting, a chapter-by-chapter approach whereby the class as a whole or in groups takes on the end-of-chapter activities constitutes one, traditional approach. Have students read and discuss each of the chapters and complete the end-of-chapter questions and activities. In this scenario, we suggest incorporating as much hands-on experience as is feasible; that is, students can develop online tasks germane to a given chapter and experiment role playing both teachers and students in assessing its value and potential for a given group of learners the task targets. Have students seek out instructional conversations in various online venues, analyze these using the text's **communication venue** affordances and share these analyses.

If the reader is solo in this enterprise, he or she can still use the chapter-by-chapter approach while rounding out the experience with more illustrations of the communication venue's uses found on the internet and or generated for and explored with an online professional development buddy. There are plenty of supportive social media groups and *blogs* for online teachers communicating with each other; exchanging their experiences, challenges and tips; and sharing new trends in the field, for example: Teachers Teaching

Online; MOOC Group for Teachers; K-12 Online Teachers; The iNACOL Network; Ultimate Support Group for Online Tutors; and Teacher Chatboards, to name a few.

Novices

If you are new to online teaching, there are scores of informative videos on YouTube with which to get one's feet wet. Our experience has been that the best way to begin learning about online instruction is to take a course. *MOOCs* can give you a general idea of structure and basic modes of interactivity. Unfortunately (because they are free), their size precludes instructors engaging online students in instructional conversations. There are simply too many students for the number of instructors. Some short courses offered by community colleges can be fairly inexpensive but again may not have sufficient investment to afford well-crafted instructional conversations (one gets what one pays for). Take a course that is valuable to you and kill two birds with one stone; gain a sense of how the online medium can be tamed for instruction while learning something you love.

The text is arranged to familiarize the reader with the different communication venues and their affordances for instructional conversations. The uninitiated can thereby immerse themselves in a wide range of practices with various groups of learners in a wide range of subjects. As you review the illustrations, imagine that you are in the teaching driver's seat making emendations that suit your particular instructional needs. In this way, the text's many examples and accompanying commentaries can come to suit your particular purposes and those of your students.

Practicing online professional educators

Our hope is that experienced online teachers will find a wealth of ideas and inspiration for expanding their expertise. By seeing the work of other online educators and considering what may be new uses of the various communication venues for your work, we aim to spark the kind of ongoing thinking and development that make great teachers the greatest. Reading straight through, chapter-by-chapter is always an option. Once familiar with the format and aims of each chapter, the text can also be accessed as a reference when you are in the process of developing activities for a specific communication venue. Regardless of the subject area illustrated and discussed, ideas for adaptation to your specific group of learners, there is inherent potential herein. For example, if the illustration teaches history to younger children, ideas to provoke and extend critical thinking and the exploration of varying perspectives can be extracted and adapted to other settings and audiences. In this way, the text can be used as an idea book for quick reference.

As is exemplified in the text's many illustrations, we adhere to a learner- and learning-centered approach to instruction. We see tasks and activities that engage learners with the content and especially *communicating* with, through and about the content as the norm in online instruction. Likewise, to reap the most benefit from this text, we encourage simultaneous *use* of these practices. Try out these conversation strategies. See what works best for you and for your students. Keep a log of what works and what doesn't. Take advantage of the archiving capacity of online teaching and examine the instructional conversations you have developed and troubleshoot. Another great advantage of online teaching is that you can *see* the learning and/or *see* where the learning should be happening and when it is not via what learners say. And by all means share these practices with your colleagues through professional organizations (see resources) and online.

Nota bene: While this text provides a comprehensive approach to instructional design and practices for online education, it is not a technical manual. The delivery devices and their software applications that your institution uses should provide that kind of information and support. In short, we do not tell you what icon to click on nor how to move things around on the screen. This text concerns pedagogy.

Format

The first chapter lays out the foundation for the subsequent chapters by providing background information on **distance education** generally and our conversation-based approach in particular. It defines and discusses communication venues and their affordances as well as instructional conversation strategies and how they work in each mode. This foundation is built upon in the second chapter through an exploration of the instructional conversation strategies *saturating* and *modeling* and how these unfold in the different communication venues to serve learning. In the third and fourth chapters, the instructional conversation strategies of **corralling, orchestrating interactions and scaffolding synthetic thinking** are likewise illustrated and discussed. Chapter 5 examines the critical role of *feedback* and the unique and important forms it can take online, while in Chapter 6 we illustrate and discuss the instructional design strategy of *content chunking* its accompanying *instructional elements*, critical components serving as the grounding for instructional conversations. In the final chapter, we look to the future of online instruction and suggest conversation-based directions.

Summary

Ultimately, our aim in developing this text is to educate those in the online teaching and learning community regarding the vital importance of instructional conversations, what and how they contribute to effective teaching and learning and the extent to which an educational professional's craft can expand when incorporating these in online instruction. The centrality of instructional conversations in effective instructional practices cannot be overstated and we are confident that readers will come to share our enthusiasm as they incorporate them in their practice.

Resources

Professional organizations

Online Learning Consortium (OLC): An international consortium of online researchers and practitioners.

Multimedia Educational Resources for Learning and Online Teaching (MERLOT): A vast repository of digital learning objects that can be freely incorporated into courses.

International Association for K-12 Online Learning (iNACOL): An organization that facilitates collaboration, advocacy and research to enhance quality K-12 online teaching and learning.

United States Distance Learning Association (USDLA): A non-profit association formed to promote the development and application of distance learning for education and training.

Online teaching providers

The Learning Resources Network (LERN): Offers information and consulting expertise to providers of continuing education and customized training.

International Council on Open and Distance Education (ICDE): Drives best practice and the highest standards of educational provision.

Online Learning Update

Coursera: Offers over 2,000 courses in various disciplines taught by top instructors from the world's best schools.

MOOC list: Locate very large but free online courses open to all.

Tools

Blendkit learning toolkit: Online educator tools.

Designing for learning: Online educator tools.

geteducated.com: Links to materials and instruction for prospective online teachers.

K12.com: Overview material of what online instruction looks like from the child's and the instructor's points of view.

LiveLesson system: Overview material of what online instruction looks like from the child's and the instructor's points of view.

Virtualelementaryschool.com: Overview material of what online instruction looks like from the child's and the instructor's points of view.

Virtualhighschool.com: Overview material of what online instruction looks like from the child's and the instructor's points of view.

1

Teaching online: a conversational approach

In this chapter you will learn:

- the nature of online instructional conversations and the specifics of their functioning in a range of online environments;

- how instructional conversations work when *Teaching with Voice*, *Teaching with Text* and *Teaching in Real Time*;

- how each environment's affordances can be optimized to support and amplify these conversations;

- the role of playfulness and humor in online teaching.

Introduction

To truly teach, one must converse; to truly converse is to teach. (Tharp and Gallimore, 1991: 4)

This chapter introduces a ***conversational approach*** to online teaching and learning, the main focus of this text. Throughout subsequent chapters, we discuss and illustrate how and why ***online instructional conversations*** can be effective for young students and rewarding for you, the instructor. In this first chapter, the rationale behind the approach and the fundamentals of online activity design and active teaching via instructional conversations are presented as they align with the goals and processes of contemporary education. We begin the chapter with an overview of the potential pedagogical merits of online and ***blended learning***.

Why online?

At the tremendously rapid rate at which online teaching and learning are being embraced worldwide, the question *Why online?* may soon be obsolete. For the moment, however, educators around the United States and worldwide are posing this question and considering carefully the rationale for offering online educational opportunities to their students.[1]

Why the rush to move learners online? This expanding migration makes good sense for a number of important reasons:

(1) Opportunity

Where there is no critical mass, as with

- less commonly taught school subjects;
- schools with small enrollments;

and for

- students whose homes are far from bricks-and-mortar schools;
- students who have physical or psychological challenges too great for bricks-and-mortar environments.

(2) Fit

Whereby

- most school-age students are accustomed to and comfortable with digital literacy through informal recreational practices;
- online instruction can be rendered developmentally appropriate, tailored and responsive to individual learners;

- the range of at-hand materials and the ways learners can interact with them to learn is limitless online.

(3) Pedagogical affordances

Where there is growing empirical evidence of

- convenience;
- connectivity;
- membership (playing field is leveled);
- authentic audiences;
- tailored audiences;
- strategies to compensate for lack of non-verbal information;
- richness of information (links, multimedia);
- time to focus and review;
- time to compose, resources to compose;
- time and opportunity to reflect;
- opportunity to witness and track learning;
- opportunity to demonstrate learning.

In short, online teaching and learning represent both excellent opportunities and fit for many learners and, as is the emphasis throughout this text, an abundance of opportunities for educators to exploit the pedagogical affordances of multidimensional online venues. The chapters that follow intend to model and guide educators as they develop and implement online learning activities in ways that complement and amplify their professional beliefs and practices, especially as these are instantiated through instructional conversations with learners.

Why instructional conversations?

Computers, especially when they serve as they most often serve nowadays – to facilitate communication between people – are highly *social machines*. Our preferred uses of computers overwhelmingly involve connecting with others: to play games, to *chat*, to compare notes, to cooperate, to agitate, to commiserate, to antagonize – activities that are very similar to those we most enjoy offline. Our current online social discourse practices have evolved organically, non-systematically, serendipitously. They continue to evolve. Computers will never possess the human capacity for making informed judgments and interpretations, never mind the capacity to take on the perspectives of interlocutors. The machine, therefore, will forever play a *supporting role* in our teaching and learning enterprises; supporting critical mediation and supplying resources used in online human conversation.

How does conversation constitute *instruction? learning?* The concept of teaching and learning as conversation differs radically from traditional notions of instruction where one individual, an instructor, is equipped with knowledge and works to transplant this knowledge into students. In short, a one-way transmission of information. Thus, the widely shared concept: *learning as transmission of information.* Sadly, this concept of teaching and learning as knowledge transmission has literally invaded our language, our conceptualizations, our bones, so much so that it has become difficult to talk and write about instruction in ways that deviate from this paradigm. One need only listen to ways the media, policymakers and the business sector talk about the educational enterprise to hear this paradigm operating alive and well. Venturing outside the safety of viewing both our instructional language practices and the ways we think and talk about technology from a critical distance is the task of this text. Here, teaching and learning are considered part and parcel of our daily in-school and out-of-school discourse practices where conversation with others across forums, mediums and technologies is the locus of learning with the deliberate shaping of the conversations constituting the teaching and the learning. Our focus throughout is on the **instructional conversation**.

First coined by Goldenberg in 1992 in the context of traditional, face-to-face teaching and learning, instructional conversation is a means of teaching that nurtures and supports learner development of understanding through talk (Goldenberg, 1992). Learners are guided to share their thinking as a means of developing it. This is done with others through speaking and writing. This kind of *responsive teaching* (Tharp & Gallimore, 1988) puts student learning and student talk in the spotlight rather than the teacher. This kind of instructional responsiveness requires flexibility, openness to others, superior listening skills and fashioning optimal instructional responses to **teachable moments**. It requires that instructors know their students and their subject matter extremely well so that these can be effectively coordinated in a fluid, ongoing manner. It also requires acute attention to **teachable moments** whereby students can be led to see and interpret their own and others' development as they move toward deep understanding, generative uses of and, ultimately, mastery of the subject area discourse.

Perspective-taking

In considering online instructional conversations, it is important to consider perspective-taking. When we read, speak, attempt to understand, we take on the perspective of the person who is either the source and/or the target of the communicating. This is a fundamental element of effective communication known widely as *theory of mind:* the understandings we are continually in the process of refining based on what and how others with whom we communicate think, believe and operate. Much of this understanding generates from the cumulative and continually edited learning we do over a lifetime of being in the world with others. Simply put, when conversing with others what we say and what we understand are shaped by our taking on one another's perspectives, of walking in one another's shoes. It is through this mutual perspective-taking that messages get negotiated. This in the moment, in one another's shoes interaction is almost always instructional in one way or another. We are not only teaching and learning about what we are talking about (the topic and informational content of our utterances), but we are also teaching and learning about how things get done with words in a socially and interpersonally successful way. We are simultaneously learning about ourselves and our relationship with the world and, to some extent, about our interlocutors and how they relate linguistically to their worlds.

Identity/identification

Our key biological inheritance is to identify with others; to see the world from their position, through their eyes, based on what we know about the world and on what we can read from the individual as we jointly construct meaningful exchanges with them. It is this unique attribute that marks us both as human and as teachers and learners; for it is perspective-taking that compels us to do both: teach and learn. Teaching and learning is, therefore, a quintessential human activity. It is speakers or writers engaging one another in such a way as to guide, inspire and experience the pleasures and rewards of minds coming together and communicating. Throughout our perspective-driven interactions with our world, we teach and we learn. When we are teaching and learning the content/substance aspect of our utterances, we are simultaneously learning new ways to think about them, to see them. If the way of thinking about what is being spoken or written about is not new but resembles our own, we are learning that our own perspective is shared and what it feels like to see eye to eye with others. If we hear the same information from the same perspective continually (memes in the echo chamber), a sense of membership is learned. Indeed, when the same information with the same perspective with the same effect is repeated often enough, it becomes a slogan and blinds its subscribers to other possibilities.

Context and mind

Considering the amount of time we spend using language with others, the depth of the experience we have while immersed in conversational interactions is vast in terms of the constant learning we do and the continual consequences on who we are and how we relate to our worlds. The extensive amount of inferencing required in verbal interaction reflects both the power of language in individual and collective agency as well as the indeterminacy of our linguistic system *per se*. Words themselves don't mean. Sentences on their own are almost always ambiguous. In short, we work with the language we use by employing our knowledge of the world in collaboration with the cumulative and dynamic ways we understand language as it is used to make meaning. Language is not in itself a way of communicating. It is but a bare tool that our intellect, social experiences and the given moment in time use to generate and understand meaning.

Affinities

As social networking genres develop, so too do genre/community-specific forms and styles of communication. We need only go on the internet to witness such developments. Sloppy though chatting and texting language may seem compared to other communities' communication norms and practices, it is, nonetheless, communication whereby we teach and learn. The communication that results is successful and, with language, that's what counts. Like all communicative venues, the quite local and particular context-building and perspective-taking that goes on in online exchanges draws on our sociolinguistic experiences and language competences. Communicating online is as interpretatively complex an activity as face-to-face interaction, if not more so in that the reading between the lines that we do in both situations is subject to the literal physicality of those lines. In the case of online conversations, infinite amounts of time to study the spaces between them do not equate with real-time non-verbal information. Nonetheless, we do this reading between the lines, employing our theory of mind well. For example, we readily repair the communicative mistakes we make through errors of interpretation. As part of our 'reading' of our interlocutors' understandings as these unfold in conversation, we also read whether our postings/utterances are being interpreted as we intended. In short, we facilely adapt our communicative predispositions to telecommunications to gain and retain membership in communities. This is a tribute to our social drive to make sense of the world through language with others regardless.

Strategies

How is it that we manage all of this? First, building mutually understood contexts is foundational to successful communication of any kind. The following are some of the understandings that we employ as we read and respond to one another's postings:

- continual assessment of what our interlocutor knows and does not know (our shared knowledge);

- complex knowing of our mutual status in the world, in the context of these exchanges, and how these may or may not change in the course of our communicating;

- jointly established sense of our context of use – the virtual, ideational context in which we communicate;

- jointly established schema for anaphoric and exophoric referents;

- mastery of language as it is generated and as it assimilates contextual nuances;

- flexible understanding of expertise as inherent and generative within the particular context of use (mastery of multiple semiotic/discourse systems; their generation and their interpretation).

We are organically and non-systematically growing online practices and, as they are taking shape, we are also teaching and learning with one another about what constitutes a responsible communicator in online communities. Although a few early attempts at rudimentary 'how-to' lists of online communication protocols appeared in the mid-nineties ('netiquette'), these were rarely read and referenced for the purpose of being a better online citizen. However, they were, for the most part, heeded; with the knowledge, skills and abilities needed to be a successful online communicator emerging organically via our predispositions as social beings. For the most part, you can go into a particular online communication site and scope out its sociolinguistic norms and conventions in fairly short order. We are creatures adept at reading social situations and doing what is needed and in keeping; to bid for and maintain membership when we choose to do so. We can readily intuit where we belong, might belong and absolutely don't belong without instruction of any kind.

These forms of social/sociolinguistic expertise are the essence of our social selves. However, they are rarely considered as foundational traits in theories and practices of education. There is, of course, the exceptional classroom where skillful instructors exploit the natural social dispositions and impetus of students to engage the learning in powerful ways. However, the legacy of psychological traditions and the objectification of learners and learning continue their influence. Where recent theoretical and practical shifts away from the individual, in the head, toward the social actor have flourished in the academic literature, these have sadly had little impact on policies such as the design of teaching and learning spaces and standardized, psychometric testing. Note that one can certainly make the case that rows of desks facing a lecturing teacher are less the norm than in earlier times and that in some enlightened corners of the testing industry assessment activities by which students demonstrate skills other than the five-paragraph essay and/or recall of objective facts have crept in.

Figure 1.1 represents the key elements that contribute to the shaping and outcomes of instructional conversation strategies as a pedagogical approach to teaching the content areas. Within the inverted cone, starting on the left is the element of *ways of knowing*. In any academic subject domain, there are specific ways of viewing and talking about the subject area. These ways of knowing are most readily apparent in the *discourse* of the materials and of those who participate as the insiders of the subject area. When we

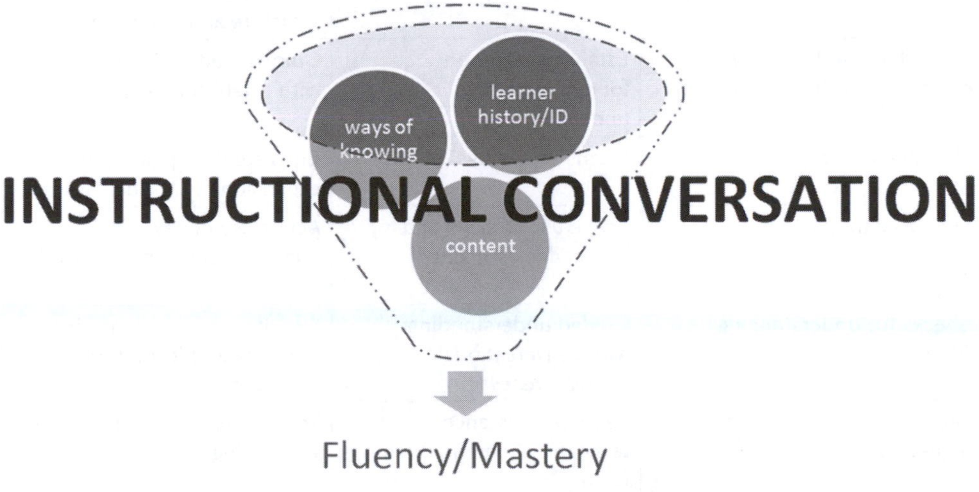

Figure 1.1 Instructional conversation

engage learners in instructional conversations, we do so as insider participants and thus model the rules and norms of that *academic discourse* community. Moving clockwise, *learners' histories and identities* come into play. Excellent instructional conversations engage learners fully. To do so, who learners are as individuals and as a group factor centrally in how instructional conversations are shaped by skilled educators. Knowing one's students is, in short, key to great teaching online or off. Finally, as you will see throughout the illustrations of online instructional conversations all through this text, *content is central*. The concepts and accompanying language of the content area form both the impetus for and the meat of instructional conversations.

Online conversations differ in many and important ways from face-to-face. Whether you teach synchronously or asynchronously or some combination of the two, the characteristics and resources of the online venue contribute to the shape of your posts and students' responses to them (Table 1.1).

Table 1.1 *Direct instruction vs instructional conversations vs online instructional conversations*

Direct instruction	Instructional conversations	Online instructional conversations
Teacher models for imitation	Teacher models for facilitation	Teacher models for active use and appropriation
Elicits exact responses	Encourages connections with background knowledge and experiences	Encourages meaningful output that elaborates and problematizes prior learning
Skills directed	Thinking directed	Development directed
Easy to evaluate	Encourages diverse performances	Ongoing assessments as part of conversation
Lockstep instruction	Sequence of instruction responsive to learners and context	Task-based sequencing within which sequencing responsive to learners
Teacher centered	Student centered	Student centered with teacher structure and guidance
Guided and independent practice following instruction	Establish common foundations for understanding	Guided student interactions with established focus
No extension/expansion	Extensive discussion	Consistent emphasis on expansion of task/discussion
Step-by-step mastery	Active use of skills and knowledge as needed	Active use of new understandings in producerly contexts
Checks for understanding (IREs)	Guided understanding with conversational responsiveness	Simultaneous guidance in meaning and form during interaction
Teacher assistance when requested	Teacher assistance at teachable moments then fading	Teacher assistance throughout with fading

Throughout the text, we will be illustrating and discussing a variety of specific online instructional conversation strategies. These are summarized as follows:

Saturating and modeling: Saturating means inundating instructional discourse throughout the online instructional venue with the targeted vocabulary and accompanying conceptualizations. Saturation is part and parcel of thoughtfully crafted instructional conversations. Similarly, modeling refers to producing models of the targeted content and skills throughout online activities. In short, words and concepts can be frequently repeated and/or modeled in instructor discourse.

Corralling: A verbal means of cornering learners into thinking and communicating in discipline-appropriate ways, thereby demonstrating authentic mastery.

Orchestrating interactions and scaffolding synthetic thinking: An *instructional conversation strategy* that renders the classroom a community of learners with both students and instructors scaffolding each other and making interactions instructional.

Providing feedback: The form of response to students as it figuratively feeds back to the learner the salience he or she needs to make sense of what is being discussed.

The following sections describe the three major formats for online instructional conversations. Of course, all of these are often combined in various ways in online courses and blended course support sites. We categorize and discuss these as Teaching with Voice, Teaching with Text and Teaching in Real Time and the affordances of each mode.

Teaching with voice

In online environments where individuals and groups can post recorded audio messages, *teaching with voice* is the instructional medium. Accompanying these audio messages can be visual and textual information. Venues for posting and sharing these multimodal messages can be almost any telecommunications medium: emails, blogs, message boards, community messaging sites, etc. For learners wishing to practice another language, there are a number of publicly accessible oral asynchronous sites whereby they can seek out tutors and conversation partners with whom to exchange multimodal messages (see end-of-chapter notes).

The difference between real time versus delayed time in online communication is vast in terms of the essential nature of the communication process. When it comes to teaching and learning in general, this difference becomes substantial; the time one has to think, assimilate and compose makes a world of difference, most notably as regards affect.

Recorded voice is an *asynchronous mode* of communication. With oral asynchronous modes, learners have the luxury of time to repeat recorded messages, access resources, thereby comprehending and strategizing their responses. In composing their responses, they can again enjoy the luxury of unlimited time with which to rehearse, record and revise their posts. Likewise, instructors can take their time to develop and construct their instructional conversation strategies in response to learners. The affordance of being able to scan, recap and repeat an audio post as many times as needed can be capitalized on to focus on challenging content. Moreover, instructors and learners can use their voice in conjunction with other modalities to draw attention to specific features using intonation. As we will see in this chapter, the asynchronous aspect, along with the oral/aural, holds numerous possibilities in this regard.

In combination with other modes, *teaching with voice* is a viable supplement especially when the emphasis is on mastering the discourse of the academic area being studied. Additionally, the oral asynchronous mode works nicely as a complement to blended courses: courses that take place partly face-to-face and partly online.

Teaching with text

Teaching and learning via *written asynchronous* text is by far the most common and preferred mode for online teaching and learning. However, even though it is technologically simple, accessible and mechanically easy to use, it nevertheless requires reconceptualization regarding teaching and learning processes, especially the critical role of *instructional conversations*. Indeed, teacher-orchestrated instructional conversations work particularly well and form the nexus of learning when *teaching with text*. Throughout this book, we illustrate and discuss such online instructional conversation strategies as these unfold in written *asynchronous environments,* a venue where instructors and students enjoy the luxury of time to fully engage teachable moments. There is no doubt that flexibility in terms of time and place, along with the fact that participation structures allow for all students to exercise equal voice, make teaching with text an attractive option.

Teaching in real time

When scheduling and other constraints allow, synchronous online teaching can also be a valuable instruction mode. This *teaching in real time* can happen in written-only or oral/aural or combined modes. Real-time text exchanges fall under the name chat or texting. Interlocutors read and type messages often to more than one person at a time. Messages appear instantaneously on the receiver's screen with all language and typographical errors intact. Thus, in many ways, written synchronous modes can be viewed as resembling real-time face-to-face interaction in that these written messages can be just as linguistically messy as they are in live interaction and, like in face-to-face talk, one must work and work hard in real time to ensure shared comprehension. The affordances of *written synchronous* environments allow learners more time to reflect on their own output, which leads to depth of processing to increase the accuracy of what they write.

Audio/video conferencing in real time can resemble face-to-face, real-time classrooms. This is an online environment whereby students can talk to each other and with their instructors using headsets or speakers and microphones with their devices. Most *oral synchronous* online environments offer the following functions: lists of participants; whiteboards for displaying and manipulating different documents; chat boxes; breakout rooms where instructors can put their students for small-group activities; and application sharing features whereby instructors and students can display the content of their desktops. Teachers and students can manipulate both uploaded files and electronic whiteboard tools. Teachers can design and conduct activities that resemble face-to-face, student–student and student–teacher interactions. Moreover, features of oral synchronous online environments that are not available in traditional classrooms such as public and individual text messaging in the chat area, breakout rooms, web application sharing and recorded archives can be very useful instructional tools. Archiving what happens in the course can be a valuable planning and assessment tool for teachers and an excellent way for students to review the content they are studying as it has been authentically discussed.

Playfulness and humor in online teaching

According to Cicero, conversation requires 'the spice of wit'. At the same time, he preferred letter writing to face-to-face interaction in so far as one can be more candid on paper. A letter, after all, 'does not blush' (Menaker, 2010: 38). Parallels with contemporary online communication are clear. *Playfulness* with the language and ideas under study invariably work to engage learners more socially and, therefore, more actively with target content. Humor, after all, has an emotional and thus a more memorable impact. Moreover, in the age of social networking and its attendant pleasures, contemporary learners are accustomed to seeking out and achieving social satisfaction while online. A sense of membership wrought from active, successful communication has become, therefore, a standard in online education.

Throughout the examples in in the following chapters, online educators use humor and playfulness to great effect. They employ visual humor, the unexpected, the groaner and the incongruous in their quest to provoke learner attention and learning. They exploit the features of various online resources to induce the 'sheer delight which seems to arise from surrender to chance and unpredictability' (Cook, 2000: 124). We encourage you to share in this delight as you observe and consider these online instructional conversations in action.

Note

(1) According to Watson *et al.* (2014), 30 American states had fully online schools. K-12 online enrollment keeps escalating drastically. 'Nationally, there is likely a total of 5,000,000–7,000,000 online enrollments in full-time and supplemental programs combined, if not more. K-12 online learning is growing at a rate that clearly outpaces the research we have about it' (Pourreau, 2015: 15).

End-of-chapter notes

Websites for online communication

https://moodle.org/

https://classroom.google.com/

https://www.coursesites.com

https://eliademy.com/

https://www.adaptiveu.io/

https://www.udemy.com/

https://www.rcampus.com/

https://appear.in/

https://www.anymeeting.com/

https://www.meetingburner.com/

http://sync.in/

http://edmodo.com/

https://padlet.com/

https://proboards.com/

End-of-chapter activities

(1) With a partner, review a single day in your life in terms of your online social interactions. Compare these communications with the face-to-face interactions you engaged in during the same period. What do you make of any similarities and differences? Is there evidence of teaching and learning going on in either venue as the chapter purports?

(2) What kinds of online learning experiences have you had? Generate a list. Compare as a group.

(3) Find a sample of conversation online. This can be from a course, a blog, the comments section on social media, wherever. Are any portions of this conversation instructional? What about *potentially* instructional? What would **you** change?

Further reading

Adelstein, D. and Barbour, M.K. (2017) Improving the K-12 online course design review process: Experts weigh in on iNACOL National Standards for Quality Online Courses. *International Review of Research in Open & Distance Learning* 18 (3), 47–82.

Barbour, M.K. and Harrison, K.U. (2016) Teachers' perceptions of K-12 online. *Journal of Educational Technology Systems* 45 (1), 74–92.

Clark, J.E. (2010) The digital imperative: Making the case for a 21st-century pedagogy. *Computers and Composition* 27 (1), 27–35.

Comas-Quinn, A. (2011) Learning to teach online or learning to become an online teacher: An exploration of teachers' experiences in a blended learning course. *ReCALL* 23 (3), 218–232.

Cope, B. and Kalantzis, M. (2009) New media, new learning. In D.R. Cole and D.L. Pullen (eds) *Multiliteracies in Motion: Current Theory and Practice* (pp. 87–103). New York: Routledge.

Goodyear, P., Salmon, G., Spector, J.M., Steeples, C. and Tickner, S. (2001) Competences for online teaching: A special report. *Educational Technology Research and Development* 49 (1), 65–72.

Gulosino, C. and Miron, G. (2017) Growth and performance of fully online and blended K-12 public schools. *Education Policy Analysis Archives* 25 (123/124), 1–38.

Meskill, C. and Anthony, N. (2007) The language of teaching well with learning objects. *Journal of Online Learning and Teaching* 3 (1), 79–93.

Rowsell, J. (2013) *Working with Multimodality: Rethinking Literacy in a Digital Age*. London/NewYork: Routledge.

Tyre, C.A. (1952) The conversational approach to language learning: An evaluation and an answer to our critics. *The Modern Language Journal* 36 (2), 59–64.

References

Cook, G. (2000) *Language Play*. New York: Oxford University Press.

Goldenberg, C. (1992) Instructional conversations: Promoting comprehension through discussion. *The Reading Teacher* 46 (4), 316–326.

Menaker, D. (2010) *A Good Talk: The Story and Skill of Conversation*. New York: Hachette Press.

Pourreau, L. (2015) Interview with Joe Freidhoff: A bird's-eye view of K-12 online learning. *Online Learning* 19 (5), 13–17.

Tharp, R. and Gallimore, R. (1988) *Rousing Minds to Life: Teaching, Learning and Schooling in Social Context*. New York: Cambridge University Press.

Watson, J., Pape, L., Murin, A., Gemin, B. and Vashaw, L. (2014) *Keeping Pace with K-12 Digital Learning 2014*. Durango, CO: Evergreen Education Group.

Saturating and modeling in online teaching

In this chapter you will learn:

- how the online instructional conversation strategies *saturating* and *modeling* work;

- how saturating and modeling work when *Teaching with Voice*, *Teaching with Text* and *Teaching in Real Time*;

- how saturating and modeling as instructional conversation strategies can be undertaken in a range of online environments;

- how saturating and modeling can be playful and humorous;

- how each environment's affordances can be optimized to support and amplify these instructional conversations.

About saturating and modeling

Two instructional conversation strategies that work extremely well in online venues are (1) saturating with text and visuals to reinforce learning and (2) modeling the target language and accompanying concepts via text and visuals. Where these strategies are also excellent in the live classroom, in online venues they can be even more effective due to the characteristics and affordances of the medium. For saturating, the fact that instructors can take the time to inundate their course screens and documents with the targeted vocabulary and their accompanying conceptualizations and thoughtfully place, review, revise and refer to these throughout, make the learning outcomes of this technique more salient than in face-to-face classes. Likewise, learners have optimal opportunities to see the target language and content *in context*. They can consider how the language and ideas are being productively used and, if they choose to do so, preserve them in a different form (a personal learning journal, for example) for later reference and review. Encountering items to be learned repeatedly in a variety of forms and in a variety of contexts augments both the understanding and the learning that take up long-term residence in the developing content area repertoire (Shuell, 1988).

As with modeling, instructors can continually produce models of the targeted content and skills throughout online activities. Learners themselves can be encouraged to provide their own models for other learners to consider with these being a rich source for stimulating and anchoring instructional conversations (Goldenberg, 1992). Both saturating and modeling represent instructional strategies that stimulate attention, actively illustrate language and concepts and, especially in online environments, become strategies to optimize learner access to and comprehension of the target content (Meskill & Anthony, 2014). Teachers and students have both the time and space to construct and comprehend visually enhanced archived instructional conversations, time and space that can be used in alignment with individual needs, preferences and convenience.

This chapter is divided into four sections. The first two, Saturating and Modeling with Voice and Saturating and Modeling with Text, involve discussion and examples of asynchronous methods for using oral and written tools for instruction. The final sections, Saturating and Modeling in Audio/Video Conferencing and Saturating and Modeling in Text Chats, examine how synchronous audio and text communication can capitalize on saturation and modeling to support and enhance learning.

Saturating and modeling with voice

We begin our discussion of the instructional techniques saturating and modeling by examining how these can be accomplished in oral asynchronous environments and/or by incorporating audio recordings into online courses or complements to courses. Posting files of one's recordings, voice, sounds, music, etc., can be easily accomplished using standard, basic digital audio tools. The advantages of doing so in terms of saturating and modeling are numerous. Again, both teachers and students can invest time and care in planning, rehearsing, reviewing and editing their course and content-focused comments and products prior to sharing these. As such, saturating recordings with focal language and ideas is greatly facilitated. Likewise, this opportunity to plan and amend one's recording makes modeling readily realizable as well.

In the next sections, we will illustrate and discuss a variety of techniques for optimizing the use of voice via saturating and modeling. We first look at making use of definitions as we saturate. This is followed by discussion and illustration of how disciplinary-specific language in use can be repeated (saturated) and modeled. Then, we turn to ways that language can be used to refer and thus anchor concepts. We end this section on the use of voice by providing examples of playfulness when saturating and modeling target content.

Saturating with definitions

A key to learning new content is repetition. The more that students actively encounter the language and the ideas they express in an active, engaged manner, the more likely they are to learn these well enough to use them actively and productively themselves. Creating voice files allows the teacher sufficient time to plan and produce oral texts that can be augmented with written texts, links, visuals and the like in order to clarify and amplify the content that learners can control and repeat as needed.

Example: Critical thinking (high school; college)

In the short introductory video on the topic of critical thinking from http://voicethread.com/share/1301729/, the teacher uses two key words: 'develop' and 'objective'. In doing so, he hammers home two major points without stating them explicitly: (1) critical thinking can be developed and (2) critical thinking involves the concept of objectivity. He stresses these two main ideas throughout this oral lecture via continuous repetition.

T: (*oral*) Critical thinking really has its genesis in the idea of being able to separate fact from fiction or truth from untruth or the false suits that exist. So it's important that students **develop** this ability and you'll **develop** this ability by being a little bit more **objective** with your reading, being little more **objective** with what you watch on television, being a little more **objective** with what you read in a newspaper and in magazines. And part of this course, an important part of this course would be to help you **develop** these things.

This example illustrates how constant repetition of the two main concepts calls learners' attention to them and establishes the focus for the entire lesson. A similar instance of saturating by definition follows.

Example: States of matter (middle school)

In this example of recorded voice, a chemistry teacher uses the words 'solids' and 'molecules' extensively in the same context. The teacher thereby focuses learner attention on two main points: (1) that the main topic of her lecture is solids and (2) that the concept of solids relies heavily on the concept of molecules. Excessive repetition of these terms in the same context helps students internalize the idea that these two constructs are strongly connected and that the concept of molecules is essential for understanding the concept of solids (Figure 2.1).

T: (*oral*) Let's talk about **solids** first. **Solids** are made up of **molecules** and those **molecules** are fairly tightly held together and they have a certain pattern in which they are held. And that makes **solids** have a definite volume and a definite shape. And what that means is that **solids** will not spontaneously grow or contract.

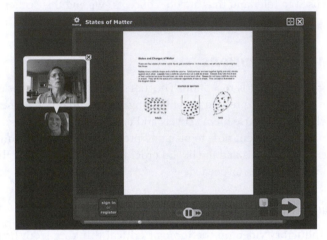

Figure 2.1 Oral saturating in VoiceThread

When using a technology such as VoiceThread, saturating can be accomplished by two modes simultaneously: written and oral. Using dual modes can be powerful as students can simultaneously listen to the instructor's utterance while reading key words denoting important concepts on the screen. Not only can the teacher saturate by oral repetition, but she can also make both meaning and form as well as important details triply redundant by incorporating multiple modalities (Figure 2.2).

Example: Sustainability (high school)

In this example, the teacher talks about environmental sustainability concepts while displaying the main ideas in text form and saturating these with the word 'responsible'. The text form of the word was subsequently noticed and pondered by a student even though the teacher did not insert it into the oral part of his instructional discourse.

T: (*oral*) I think a lot of communities exist geographically but not in any real functional organizational sense and identifying goals especially with regards to sustainability would be great first way to start to categorize priorities for all these little projects that you could do to indeed beat on the way toward the sustainability as a community.

S: (*oral*) There was a word you used here that is very powerful, which is '**responsibility**'. I think that some wealthy communities meet to take that into a more personal account because by them having all the resources to themselves um I think they need to understand that they have more **responsibility** in what their part should be um other people are able to have those resources and to have them for the long term.

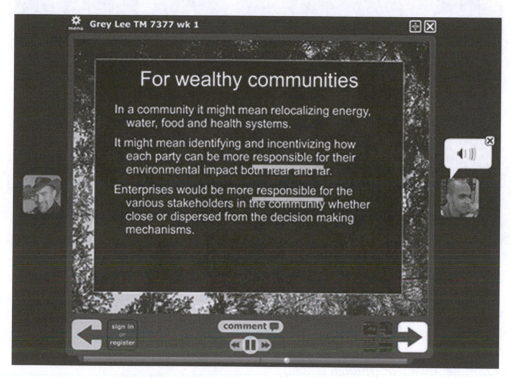

Figure 2.2 Oral and textual saturating in VoiceThread

For teachers, it is crucial not only to teach students domain-specific discourse but also to teach them general academic discourse or *the language of school* as well. Making reference to sources and providing links to relevant information is just such a feature of augmented instructional conversations. In this example, the teacher models this form of instructional talk aurally and then in text form by providing links, an increasingly pervasive and effective discourse practice in online teaching and learning. He models this on every slide to reinforce (Figure 2.3).

Example: Third-grade class follows the 2008 Iditarod

T: (*written*) To learn more about Lance Mackey go to his website at *lancemackey.com/*

T: (*written*) To learn more about Martin Buser go to his website at http://www.buserdog. com/statpage/index.html.

T: (*written*) To learn more about Jeff King check out his website at www.huskyhomestead. com.

To learn more about Martin Buser go to his website at http://www.buserdog.com/stat page/index.html

Third Grade Class Follows the 2008 Iditarod (4/23)

sign in or register

comment

Figure 2.3 Modeling academic discourse in VoiceThread

Saturating and modeling with anchors

Saturating in oral asynchronous venues can be powerful when spoken utterances are anchored to plentiful online educational resources.

Example: Civil war (middle school)

For example, one source for all subject areas is brainpop.com. This resource offers nearly a thousand cross-curricular animated movies and supporting features. Movies can be easily embedded into or linked to your voicethread. If, for example, the topic of the voicethread is the Civil War, students can watch and analyze short movies on this subject that is itself saturated with subject-specific words and phrases. These can then be repeated (re-saturated) by the instructor via both voice and text (Figure 2.4).

Character: (*oral*) The North lost of major **battles** at the beginning. Most historians think this is because the South had brilliant generals such as Robert E. Lee. One of the biggest earliest victories for the South was The First **Battle** of Bull Run.

Figure 2.4 Saturating and modeling with multiple references/anchors in VoiceThread

Playfulness

Playful saturating can be both salient and humorous. Students of all types tend to respond favorably to word play and the making of jokes as part of instructional conversations. Here, a psychology instructor has some fun with the brain.

Example: Mnemonics for the parts of the brain

In this example, the teacher uses the same word or structure several times in a humorous context to help students attend and internalize. He puts a bell on top of his head and

Figure 2.5 Playful saturating and modeling in VoiceThread

repeats the word 'cerebellum' many times, emphasizing the similarity between the word cerebellum and the word bell as well as the concept of brain and balance (Figure 2.5).

T: (*oral*) **Cerebellum**. That ain't too hard. Right in the middle of **cerebellum** a bell, right? (*sound of a bell ringing*) The **cerebellllum**. **Cerebellum** is involved with balance and motor control. And so you have to think about is that what I do is what lots of books refer to athletes and athletic ability associated with **cerebellum**. So what you could do is you could imagine in athletes that you think a lot about and someone you are fan of is that this person has lots of bells. So picture bells may be hanging off that person. Associate bell with an athlete, may be a dancer, may be someone who walks across vilpes and go to a building and a balance involved there. And that would help you with **cerebellum**.

Playful saturating and modeling can also be accomplished by using characters to make learning more fun. Programs such as Voki available from http://www.voki.com or Blabberize from http://blabberize.com/ supply speaking representatives to help learners visualize what is said.

Example: English vocabulary (middle school)

The following instance of using Voki in an online portion of a middle school English class illustrates how to make learning new vocabulary fun and engaging. The assignment was to find an intriguing word, provide a definition and some examples for it and give a short presentation of this word using the Voki device (Figure 2.6).

Figure 2.6 Playful saturating and modeling with Voki

T: (*written*) You will need to create a Voki character – any character – and one Vocab word. Please DEFINE the word and USE IT IN A SENTENCE. Maybe tell a little more about this word – what do you like about it? Also synonyms and antonyms. Be creative. Find your name and paste your Voki in the correct cell. Here is my example. (*oral*) One of my favorite words that I ran across recently is **spilth**.
       S-P-I-L-T-H. It is a noun and it's the act or an instance of spilling, something that spilled. So I could use it in a sentence. A **spilth** of water fell from the bridge speeder as a bird took a bath. **Spilth**. Try and use it today.

S1:   (*oral*) Hi. I chose the word '**cryptic**'. It means 'puzzling' or 'mystifying'. It is a bit **cryptic** that I am a talking horse. Ha-ha! Good bye!

S2:   (*oral*) **Calamitous**. **Calamitous** is an adjective meaning 'misfortune' or 'fatal'. In 1906, a **calamitous** earthquake came to San Francisco.

S3:   (*oral*) **Levity** is a lack of seriousness or earnestness. His **levity** at this serous meeting was unnecessary.

Many students in this example not only provided definitions and examples of the target vocabulary items but also illustrated them via their choice of Voki characters, thus supplying the class with short mnemonic mini-lessons.

Example: Paul Revere (middle school)

Blabberize can also be used to implement the saturating strategy in student projects. Blabberize is an applet allowing the mouths on uploaded pictures to move, creating the effect of a video with a character telling a story. This can create a sense of presence of historical figures, for instance, as in this student presentation on Paul Revere (Figure 2.7).

Paul Revere talks about his midnight ride.
By: Steven

Important points to remember about Paul Revere
- Paul Revere worked as a silver smith in the American Revolution.
- He also helped up the alarm systems to keep watch of British military.

Figure 2.7 Playful saturating and modeling with Blabberize

S: (*oral*) My name is Paul Revere and I worked as a silver smith and I was a patriot of the American Revolution in December of 1735. I was a messenger in the battles of Lexington and Concord. During that time I was a Boston craftsman who had an organization of intelligence and alarm system to keep watching on the British military. One night on April 18th to 19th, I was a messenger on a horse.

This presentation about an historical figure, saturated with historical facts and told from the first person creates a sense of immediacy; a real man talking about himself and important events in his life. Saturating in such a playful manner keeps learners engaged and prompts them to listen to this text again.

Student projects can be an excellent source of saturating and modeling techniques, especially when they are done in a playful and humorous manner (Figure 2.8).

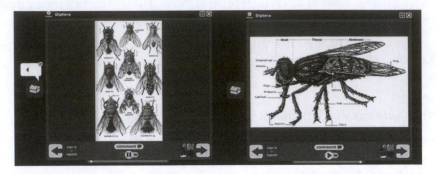

Figure 2.8 Playful modeling and saturating through student projects

Example: Diptera (middle school)

P: (*oral*) (*singing as rap*) This is **diptera** or the only true fly the interesting creature now we'll tell you why.
Last classification you need to be aware of is for – look at look at – **diptera**.
Diptera has twenty hundred thousand species.
Most transmit the textuas diseases.
Mosquitoes, necks, flies and messures
Can often be found in a matter of inches.

Now we'll fit a bit more specific.
Take notes fast 'cause it will be quick.
On a **mesa thorax** it's a single pair of wings.
On a **meta thorax** it's a pair of **pulvillies** things.
Flies were adopted to air movement.
Also there are not teeth to consume it.
They have a mobile head with **compound** eyes
The **antennas** are short and produce drugs when they fly.
The **wings** obviously keep flies in the air.
The **halters** keep them balanced there.

These two students saturated their rap song about a diptera with the term itself and also with many additional target biological terms. When done in a playful manner, such activities serve to engage learners in active, productive use of the target content.

Saturating and modeling with voice: section summary

As we have seen in this section's illustrations, saturating and modeling via voice can be powerful instructional strategies for online teaching and learning. Where these instructional conversation strategies alone in oral recorded form take good advantage of the online medium, they become even more interesting and salient for learners when accompanied by corresponding text, definitions and anchors such as links and references, and when they are carried out in a playful or humorous manner. In the next section, we explore how saturating and modeling can be accomplished in asynchronous written form.

Saturating and modeling with text

Saturating and modeling in written asynchronous formats can take the form of written text in discussion boards, blogs, emails or any other written asynchronous venue. Like teaching with recorded voice, teaching asynchronously with text has a number of pedagogical advantages. Again, instructors have time to plan, prepare, draft and revise their instructional conversation strategies responding to learners in strategic ways that are unavailable in real time. That extra time to plan, consider and compose is, of course, also available to learners, elements that can make a tremendous difference in the quality of their instructed experiences. Moreover, those portions of online courses where the instructor and/or students retain transcripts of the instructional conversations can be used quite productively for strategic planning, evaluation and review.

Saturating and definitions

Example: DNA mutation

In the following asynchronous instructional conversation, the topic is DNA. The instructor saturates the asynchronous messages with the target term 'mutation'. The repetition of this key term as a natural part of the online conversation can saliently focus learner attention while contributing to their acquisition of the term as part of their developing DNA knowledge repertoire. Instructional conversations can be saturated with both the target term and its collocations – the words that 'co-locate' with the target term such as 'DNA mutation' in the example. Saturating then reinforces students' conceptual/linguistic acquisition of target terms and phrases.

T: What is a DNA **mutation**? Explain at least 4 different types of DNA **mutations**. How do these **mutations** affect protein production? What can be the results in the cell and in the body?

S: A DNA **mutation** is any change to a strand of DNA which is passed on to an organism's offspring. Four different types of DNA **mutations** are deletion, substitution, duplication, and translocation.

In this example, the teacher models the target discourse by saturating her initial statement with the focal term. Students eagerly adopt this same strategy in their responses.

Saturating and modeling with structured answers

Example: Idioms (elementary school)

Often, teachers, especially at the elementary level, provide structured models to help their students be on-topic with their answers and to avoid digressions. Such structures set expectations and the tone for further discussions (Figure 2.9).

Figure 2.9 Saturating and modeling with structured answers in discussion forums

T: (*written*) Take the time to list your favorite saying or expression here! **Define an idiom** and **use it correctly** in a **short (but creative) paragraph**. Use at least **4 descriptive adjectives** to make your writing more interesting. Here are some of my favorites... can you figure them out based on the literal pictures?

T: (*written*) Don't look a gift horse in the mouth.
      Definition: When you get an unexpected gift or chance, don't ask questions about it. Just be happy for what you have.
      Story: Last Tuesday, pupils in Mrs Perry's wonderful reading class signed up to do presentations on Thursday and Friday. On Wednesday afternoon, right before students went home, Mrs Perry gave them a half sheet of paper with a revised schedule on it. Students were not going to even start presentations till Friday! When Tori came up and asked, 'Mrs Perry, is this really true? Do I really get the weekend to practice?' Mrs Perry said, 'Don't look a gift horse in the mouth!'

S: (*written*) Play it by ear – to not know what to expect and deciding what to do as we go along story – We were at my dad's apartment when we saw a guy working on the pool. My dad started wondering when he would get the pool passes. Then we saw the activities director, we asked her when the pool passes would come out. She didn't know, so my dad just told me, 'Let's play it by ear'.

Saturating and modeling with anchors

New interactive technologies allow saturating and modeling in online discussion that include references to multiple sources such as research and news articles, videos, flash self-quizzes, simulations and the like. Incorporating these anchors into the conversation can make learning more effective as learners can opt to go deeper when they have the time and inclination to do so.

Example: Do aye-ayes see in color? (biology blog)

In this example, the presentation about an animal was saturated with links to various sources such as YouTube videos, Science Daily, National Geographic and an online encyclopedia, which, in turn, modeled the use of this word in different contexts (Figure 2.10).

Figure 2.10 Saturating and modeling with references/anchors in discussion forums

Saturating and modeling with embedded images and audio

Saturation in discussion forums can be augmented with images embedded right in the body of the discussion. Such images can be supplied in order to support an idea or provide an additional visual reference, thereby guiding students to attend to targeted vocabulary more intensely. Saturation in discussion forums can take place via two channels simultaneously: oral and written with oral components supplementing or highlighting the written dialogue. One simple method that students find engaging is to amplify oral monologues using animated characters. Voki available from http://www.voki.com or Blabberize from http://blabberize.com/ are two online venues whereby such animations can be implemented.

Example: Animal Farm *by George Orwell (middle and high school)*

The following is an example of using Voki in a lesson plan for the novel *Animal Farm*. The Voki recording is an example of how technology can be used to model expected outcomes in student projects or discussion forums (Figure 2.11).

T: (*oral*) I'm the Cat in *Animal Farm*. I'm lazy and like to do whatever I want. I voted on both sides of the election and make false promises. I also disappear before the purges. I represent the selfish upper class of Russians who supported communism and who exploited it before it became inconvenient.

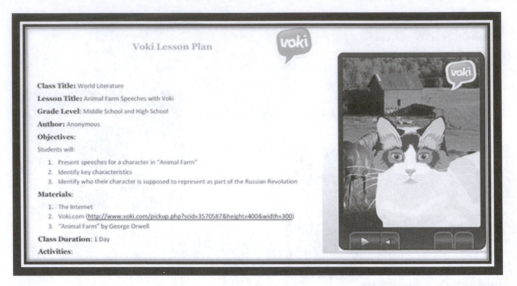

Figure 2.11 Saturating and modeling with Voki

The teacher modeled an initial post saturating it with the manner and language that she would like her students to use in their own postings: for example, 'I represent...'. The Voki voice device is an excellent tool to make a text-based discussion more colorful. Saturating and modeling the target discourse is also a productive way to draw learners' attention to what is to be actively appropriated and used. This approach in its various technical interpretations is exploited by many online teachers. Screencast building programs such as Screencast-O-Matic from http://www.screencast-o-matic.com/ can be an excellent utility for adding these kinds of modeling and saturating oral components.

Example: Language class (elementary school)

In this example, an online Russian teacher establishes a discussion forum on the topic of family members, focusing on specific grammatical aspects of students' posts, such as the gender of nouns and possessive pronouns. Students can play back this short form-focused video from any place in their discussion forum and refer to it as many times as they need to (Figure 2.12).

T: (*oral; in Russian*) My or your Mom, sister, or female friend. My or your Dad, brother, or male friend.

S: (*written; in Russian*) My brother is a student. What is your brother, John?

Another effective way to implement saturating and modeling is to do so with the help of your students who can set examples and establish standards for the rest of the class. In the following Algebra class blog, the teacher included examples of how certain algebraic problems can be solved by using videos of students modeling how to solve the problems (Figure 2.13).

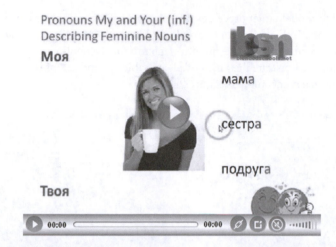

Figure 2.12 Saturating and modeling with screencasts in discussion forums

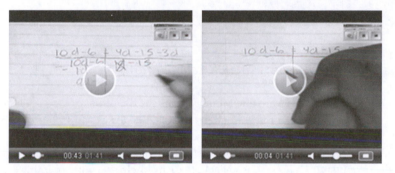

Figure 2.13 Saturating and modeling by students in discussion forums

Example: Multistep equations (middle school algebra)

T: (*written*) Remember that you should simplify what you can when you do these problems. If you see that you need to **distribute**, do so. If you see that you need to **combine like terms** at the beginning of a problem do so. The videos below demonstrate how to solve some **multi step equations**. These are student created explanations.

S: (*video*) (*oral*) 10d **minus** 6 **equals** 4d **minus** 15 **minus** 3d. First, I wanna make my **table**. Then I go by d-terms and gonna **combine like terms** 4d and **negative** 3d. We gonna make this: 1d **minus** 15. I will **bring this down**: 10d **minus** 6. Then I wanna **cancel** this 1d with the **negative** d. When I do it at **one side**, I have to do it at **another side**. It will be 9d **minus** 6 and the **negative** 15. Then I wanna come do the **like terms**, so I gonna **add** 6 to **cancel** this and **add** 6. So when I do this, I will come with 9d. I do some **addition** and this will be **negative** 9. Then you wanna get it to **the simplest terms**.

Having students model learning processes is a technique that supports both the viewing/listening aspect as well as confidence from observing peers. Similarly, student projects can also be used to model target processes and products. This works particularly well in online environments. In the following example, in his math class blog the teacher shared projects made by his students via the site http://goanimate4schools.com/public_index. The students' projects illustrate the kinds of pleasurable collaborations and learning outcomes this approach encourages (Figure 2.14).

Figure 2.14 Encouraging interactions in discussion forums

Example: Math class projects (middle school math)

T: (*written*) Class projects were due Monday. Some of the projects were really interesting. Particularly some of the animations. It was nice to see the amount of effort that was put into these projects. This is an example.

S: (*animation called Scientific Notations; includes two characters: a policeman and a man on the street*) (*oral*) (*Policeman is saying*) Hey, can I help you with anything? (*Man is saying*) Yeah, you can, mister. What a **scientific notations** and how to you use it? (*Policeman is saying*) A **scientific notation** is made for expressing a given **quantity** as a **number having certain digits**. (*The example appears on the blackboard*) (*Man is saying*) Yeah! That's a good example but how did you get the answer? (*Policeman is saying*) Well, first I did 10 to the **power** of 2 or 10 **square** which **equals** to 100. Then I **multiplied** it to 5.90. So, as a result that **equals to** 590.00.

This model is effective on several levels. First, it models subject- and topic-specific terms for the rest of the class. Second, when modeling is done by a teacher, students might involuntarily try to emulate the teacher's model assuming that this is the only *right* way to deal with the assignment. Student modeling can break this cycle. As one teacher reports: 'this form of modeling is what I often discuss as being detrimental to creativity because students will do what will please the teacher, based on what they saw, instead of taking the project in their own direction and being challenged to think and design'. In this way, student modeling can spark peer creativity and resourcefulness. Third, modeling done by students lacks authoritative power and, hence, renders what students subsequently produce more acceptable. It sets a good example and triggers healthy competence among students to explore alternative ways to complete the assignment.

Saturating and modeling with podcasts

Instructional interactions often take the form of combined modalities. For example, a teacher initiates an asynchronous instructional conversation via blogs accompanied by complementary *podcasts* with students encouraged to converse both via written comments and oral presentations or dialogues. An example of using podcasts embedded in the class blog to saturate and model content follows (Figure 2.15).

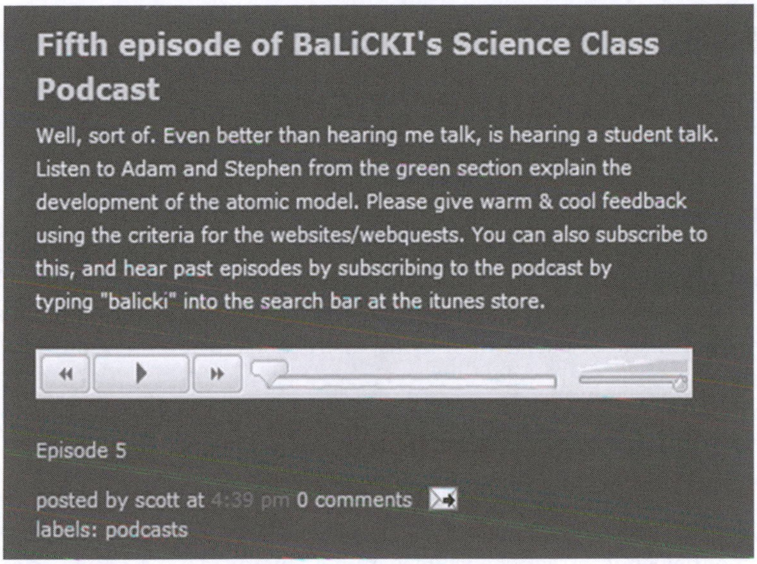

Fifth episode of BaLiCKI's Science Class Podcast

Well, sort of. Even better than hearing me talk, is hearing a student talk. Listen to Adam and Stephen from the green section explain the development of the atomic model. Please give warm & cool feedback using the criteria for the websites/webquests. You can also subscribe to this, and hear past episodes by subscribing to the podcast by typing "balicki" into the search bar at the itunes store.

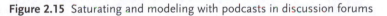

Episode 5

posted by scott at 4:39 pm 0 comments

labels: podcasts

Figure 2.15 Saturating and modeling with podcasts in discussion forums

Example: Science class podcast (chemistry blog)

T: (*written*) **Even better than hearing me talk, is hearing a student talk**. Listen to Adam and Stephen from the green section explaining the development of the atomic model.

S1: (*oral*) Schrödinger then used quantum mechanics to prove that electrons move. He thought electrons occupy 3D space so Schrödinger's get the electrons three coordinates: principle denoted N, angular denoted L, and magnetic denoted M which are all quantum numbers.

S2: (*oral*) Let me take over for a little bit. I love when we get to the quantum because you listen to Quantum Radio. So the principle quantum numbers describe the side of the orbital and the energy of the orbital. The angular describe the shape of the orbital. And the magnetic describe the position in space of their particular particles.

Saturating and modeling with text: section summary

Communicating via asynchronous text has a number of powerful affordances when it comes to teaching and learning. The extra time and resources that both teachers and students can utilize to their advantage as well as the ability to archive and make use of instructional conversations are among the most pedagogically relevant aspects of the communication mode, especially when it comes to saturating and modeling target content. Further, as we have extensively illustrated, integrating multimedia components can amplify these text-based conversations to great effect. In short, saturating and modeling with text in online and blended learning environments make good sense as instructional techniques.

Saturating and modeling in audio/video conferencing

Live audio and video conferencing whereby teachers and students interact in real time via voice and/or video also provides excellent opportunities to visually and aurally model and saturate the instructional conversation with target content. Any number of resources can be called up as foci and complements to the conversation. Unlike asynchronous modeling and saturating, however, resources must be located in advance of the live session so as not to break the rhythm and use valuable time. Thus, instructional planning prior to audio/video conferencing sessions is vital.

Saturating with target definitions

Saturating in audio/video conferences is often done with images uploaded to a common whiteboard with teachers explaining basic concepts displayed schematically in those images. Using the pen feature of the whiteboard tool, instructors can draw circles, lines and arrows to call learner attention to the subject-specific targeted linguistic and visual items, making these more salient and thus memorable (Figure 2.16).

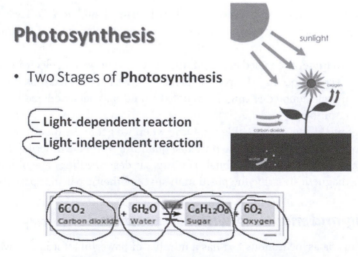

Figure 2.16 Saturating with visuals in audio/video conferences

Example: Cellular energy (middle school science)

T: (*oral*) So, let's talk about an overview of **photosynthesis**. The key terms you'd need to know are a **carbonate oxide** which comes from us. Plants need water. We need sunlight, of course. The sunlight comes from through here. It's kind of a **catalyst** is it what makes it happen. And the last but not least, the plant produces sugar which needs to grow and produces **oxygen** which is very beneficial to us. There are two reactions in **photosynthesis**. There is **light-dependent** meaning they have to have some light and **light-independent** and these **reactions** can happen in the dark.

As we can see, in this example oral saturation was amplified by the textual cues on the slide making it doubly salient and meaningful.

The terms can be saturated in several channels including the voice. Text on the slide is called attention to via circling, underscoring and web resources (Figure 2.17).

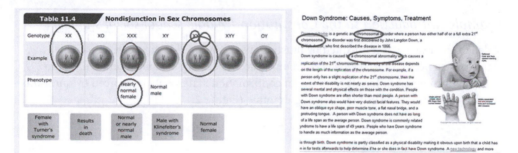

Figure 2.17 Saturating with visuals and web resources in audio/video conferences

Example: Chromosomes (middle school science)

T: (*oral*) We have **chromosomes** of a female, two Xs but a **chromosome** of a male too. In this case they actually look like a male but they have an extra **chromosome** like females do. There is some weird stuff here. That doesn't happen all that often when somebody gets an extra **chromosome** that shouldn't happen. Now I would like you to launch this web site about the Down Syndrome. It's when they get an extra 21st **chromosome**. So check out this web site really quickly. Let me launch it for you. Here is the picture of a karyotype. In the red circle, there are three **chromosomes** there and this is what we are talking about. This is when someone gets an extra set of **chromosomes**.

Instructional delivery venues offer a variety of tools for adding visuals to lessons thereby facilitating saturation and modeling techniques.

Example: Driving (middle school)

In this example, the teacher uses arrows to indicate the places to which the terms he is saying pertain (Figure 2.18).

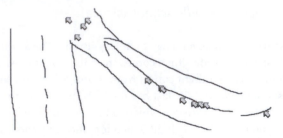

Figure 2.18 Saturating with visuals in audio/video conferences

T: (*oral*) I'm going to show you real quick what those would look like. We have the **traditional road** here. And the **entrance** coming this way. So the **entrance** is where you will enter right here, right? The **acceleration** will be right through here and the **emerging area** is up here.

Example: Introduction to the Constitution (middle school social studies)

Video of the teacher accompanied by illustrations of the mini-lecture can help create teacher presence. Like in the live classroom, teachers can model and saturate the same target definitions in different contexts: in confirmation statements reinforced by questions presented on a slide as in the following example (Figure 2.19).

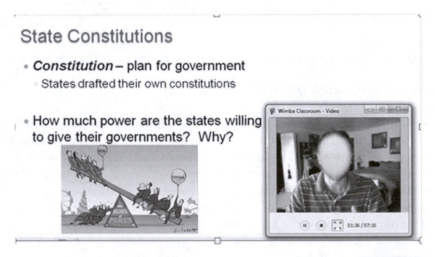

Figure 2.19 Saturating with written questions in audio/video conferences

T: (*oral*) Each state had a **constitution** already by this point but what we're trying to do remember we're the United States of America. So it's not going to be enough to have just individual states that basically how it was under the colonies. We're bringing it all together so that the state **constitutions** are applying into a federal general or a national **constitution** combining all these states together but the problem is we're not going to give a lot of **power** to the **central authority**. So what we ended up saying is that lots of states were dragging their feet really trying to put up breaks on this because they did not want a strong **central authority**, a strong **central government**. So this illustration at the bottom here we have a **balance of power** between the local and **central government**. But we also have a **balance of power** within a government itself. (*written*) State Constitutions. Constitution – plan for government. States drafted their own constitutions. How much power are the states willing to give their governments? Why?

Combining oral explanations with written questions that repeat the target terminology is a particularly effective strategy when accomplished through multiple modalities. Also, this kind of oral saturating amplified with textual models can arise quite spontaneously in audio/video conferencing classes. When this happens, the text chat section of a program can be used to support this strategy. In the following example, the teacher worked around the word 'metadrama' by saturating her oral monologue with this item and by typing it into the chat box to make it immediate for students.

Example: Shakespeare's Hamlet (high school)

T: (*oral*) If you remember from the Hamlet Trailer, it's called a revenge tragedy. Now, a revenge tragedy has a few extra characteristics that distinguish it from a regular tragedy. So, in Hamlet, we can see all these characteristics. So we see a hesitating revenger, a villain, complex plotting, murders, characters of noble birth – this is really important, a play within a play called often a **metadrama**... You should make notes on this. So remember a play within a play is often referred to as a **metadrama**, and I'll type this term into the chat box. (*written*) **Metadrama**.

Attending repeatedly to the same highlighted term in different modes of communication helps students make this targeted information part of their developing repertoires. This is especially important when misunderstanding or confusion happens with regard to focal terms as in the following example (Figure 2.20).

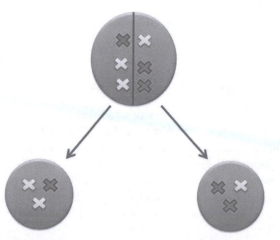

Figure 2.20 Persistent saturating in two channels in audio/video conferences

Example: Biology (high school)

T: (*oral*) OK, I'm looking for a specific gene now. Let's say it's a gene for eye color. Here it is, on that pair of chromosomes. **The location of a particular gene on a chromosome is called locus, genetic locus.** So I'm looking here for a gene for eye color and what I want to do is...

S: (*written*) did you say **focus**???

T: (*oral*) Oh I see! (*with stress*) **LOCUS. LOCUS.** I will type this word into the chat area. Take a look. (*written*) **LOCUS** (*oral*) **Genetic locus is the location of a gene on a chromosome.** (*written*) **Genetic locus is a location of a gene on a chromosome.** (*oral*) The plural form of **locus** is **loci, genetic loci** (*written*) **loci.**

In the next example, after teaching a lesson on measurement units, the teacher uses the program's built-in quiz maker not only to test students' understanding of the material but also to visually saturate responses with the terms that were attended to frequently during his oral presentation.

Example: Measurements (middle school) (Figure 2.21)

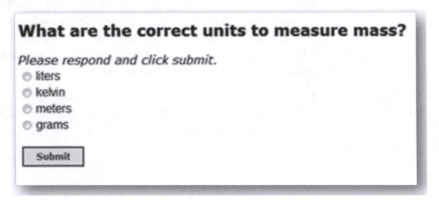

Figure 2.21 Saturating with tests in audio/video conferences

Example: Chemical bonds (middle school chemistry)

In this example, saturating and modeling with target terms happen simultaneously in two channels: verbal and written with the written models duplicated by the teacher's writing on the slide. In addition, saturating and modeling occur on two levels: the scientific key terms and analogies from students' everyday life with which they are already familiar. This is done to call students' attention to the key terms. Prior to the audio conferencing lesson, students were directed to the websites incorporating the YouTube video and short cartoons containing analogies between types of chemical bonds and bonds between dogs (Figures 2.22 and 2.23).

Figure 2.22 Saturating with terms and analogies in audio/video conferences

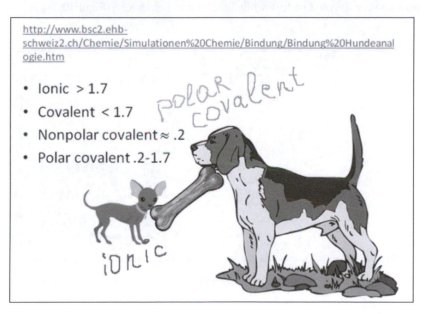

Figure 2.23 Saturating in two channels on two levels in audio/video conferences

T: (*oral*) Look at these two lovely **dogs**. What do you think they symbolize in terms of **chemical bond**? What kind of **bond**?

S1:   (*written*) **ionic**.

S2:   (*written*) **iconic**?

S3:   (*oral*) **Ionic**.

T: (*oral*) Yes, that's true. (*writes the word 'ionic' on the slide*) And why do you think it is so?

S2:   (*oral*) The **big dog** will fight the **small doggy** and take this **bone** away from him.

T: (*laughing*) (*oral*) And what is the **bone** in **chemical** terms?

S2:   (*oral*) **Electrons**?

T: (*oral*) Right! The **big dog** gets the **bone** or an **electron** acting not very nicely, he becomes **negative**. The little doggy loses the fight for an **electron** or a **bone**. He's positive. They both are still holding that bone. If the **dogs** share the **bone** but the **bigger dog** has more to eat, he gets the bigger piece of a **bone**, that would look like a **polar covalent bond**. (*writes 'polar covalent' on the slide*) Now take a look at these numbers. If the difference between their **electron negativities** is greater than 1.7 (*underscores 1.7 on the slide*), we call it the **iconic chemical bond**. OK? If that difference is less than 1.7 (*underscores 1.7 one more time*), the **bond** is **covalent**.

Example: Physics and informatics (high school and college)

In the following example, saturation takes place via three channels simultaneously. While the teacher is talking to the class, his smartboard-based lecture is displayed on the slide using an application sharing feature. Students can simultaneously listen to him talking and see the formulas both on the magnified slide and directly on the smartboard. They see the big picture and the detailed picture while listening to the lecture (Figure 2.24).

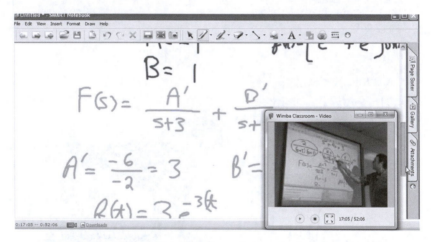

Figure 2.24 Saturating in three channels in audio/video conferences

T: (*oral*) **3e** to the what? You can go and put **t** and remember that everywhere you would've had a **t**, you have **t minus 2** 'cause it would handle it in two seconds. Remember that you gotta go back and see that it was **e to the negative 2s**. Right?

Saturation with students' modeling

Teachers frequently use students to model certain terms as in the following example from a Japanese class. The teacher intensely saturated the lesson with target nouns denoting facial features. This served as the *task toolkit* to be referred to in the subsequent communicative activities (Figure 2.25).

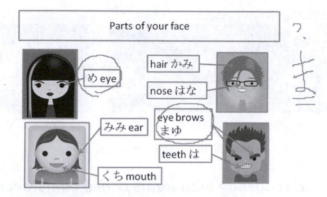

Figure 2.25 Saturating with student models

Example: Japanese language and culture (middle school)

T: (*oral*) What is the word for (*circles the word 'eye' on the slide*) 'eye'? Raise your hand.
S1:   (*written*) ma
T: (*oral*) It's not 'ma'. Student 2?
S2:   (*oral*) Me.
T: (*oral*) Me. OK. And what about (*circles the word 'ear' on the slide*) 'ear'?
S1:   (*oral*) Mimi.
T: (*oral*) Mimi! OK. Mouth (*circles the word 'mouth'*)?
S3:   (*oral*) Kuchi.
T: (*oral*) Kuchi. Right!

For language teachers, it is common to duplicate student models to make saturation more focused. This teacher also intensified saturation in the following activity, making sure her students were fluent with the use of the common nouns expressing facial features (Figure 2.26).

T: (*oral*) Do you remember how to ask 'What is it?'?
S1:   (*written*) nan des ka
S2:   (*written*) nandeska
S3:   (*written*) na n de su ka
T: (*oral*) Nan desu ka. All right! I'm going to turn on my camera. (*turns on her web camera and points to her hair*) Nan desu ka?
S3:   (*oral*) Kame.
T: (*oral*) Kami. Kami des. Nan desu ka? (*points to her nose*)
S1:   (*oral*) Hona des.
T: (*oral*) OK, now you will ask each other. Student 4, take your camera and ask the person below you. Then that person asks the person below.
S4:   (*oral*) Nan desu ka? (*points to his hair*)
S5:   (*oral*) Kami des. (*points to her eyebrow*) Nan desu ka?
S6:   (*oral*) Mayu.
T: (*oral*) Mayu des, right?

Figure 2.26 Intensive focused saturating

Saturating and modeling with audio/video conferencing: section summary

Research on learning through multiple modalities supports the common-sense observation that the more modalities engaged (1) the more salient the information and the educational experience and (2) the more options learners have to make meaning. Given audio/video conferencing whereby learners can engage well-orchestrated visual and aural information simultaneously, the instructional conversation strategies of saturating and modeling readily augment the learning experience. By seeing text and images while interacting with instructors and classmates in real time, with key content repeated and highlighted throughout, learners are motivated to attend to, engage and thereby learn the target content.

Saturating and modeling in text chats

Text-based chatting has its own particular affordances when it comes to effectively employing the instructional conversation strategies of saturating and modeling key content. Indeed, it could readily be argued that by experiencing subject-specific terminology in its textual, writ *academic*, context, learners are also acquiring understanding of how this terminology lives beyond the word level. Moreover, their own use of the new language in response to instructor and student saturating and modeling occurs in real time, thus affording opportunities for authentic, active comprehension and use of the new language. Unlike the fast-paced, ephemeral language of the live classroom, however, text chats can be read, re-read, archived, edited and revisited for study and evaluation purposes. If such files have instantiations of modeling and saturating, the target content can be reviewed readily and effectively for these purposes.

Persistent saturating

The following excerpt is from a math-focused text-based chat. The excerpt illustrates how the teacher pushed learners in the desired direction by providing two key words: equality and inequality. He saturated his responses throughout with these two terms thus guiding students through the steps to answer his initial question. This saturation is more visible to students given the written nature of the medium and, hence, more easily attended to.

Example: Math jams (middle school math)

T: (*written*) What is the greatest real number that is at least as large as its square?

T: (*written*) (*after having received wrong answers*) How do we solve such an **inequality**? Solve: $x \geq x^2$.

S1:   (*written*) Dividing by x.

T: (*written*) That might not work because x could be 0. Also if x is negative, that would change the direction of the **inequality** sign (try it and see).

S2:   (*written*) quadratics?

T: (*written*) Let's begin by looking at where the condition of **equality** holds. Where do we have **equality**?

S3:   (*written*) We have **equality** at x=0 and x=1.

S4:   (*written*) x=1, or 0.

T: (*written*) Any number of methods allow us to see we have **equality** at x=0 and x=1. Now how does this inform our approach to the **inequality**?

S3:   (*written*) 0>=x(x–1) by factoring after subtracting.

S1:   (*written*) 0>=x^2+x\nfactor x out so 0>=x(x+1).

T: (*written*) By finding the two solutions to the **inequality** we have split the number line into three regions. A quick inspection of a test case in each region reveals that the **inequality** holds between 0 and 1. 0 $\leq x \leq 1$. We could in fact reformulate the **inequality** in order to view it as a graph. We can subtract x from both sides of the **inequality** and get the equivalent **inequality**. 0 $\geq x^2 - x$. We now see that we are comparing the graph of x^2–x with 0. 0 is simply the y-axis and so we can see that only values of x between 0 and 1 inclusive satisfy the given **inequality**. This idea of graphing an **inequality** can come in very handy for quadratic **inequalities** such as this one as well as other **inequalities** that include absolute values or high degree polynomials.

The terms 'equality' and 'inequality' saturate the teacher's utterances to alert students that this concept is a key to solving the problem. Because these terms are presented repeatedly and in written form, they become more visible and, hence, central to the learning experience.

Saturating with references/anchors

In the following example of a chat on the topic of water chemistry, the teacher/tutor provides background information on the subject with his text-based discourse saturated with key water chemistry vocabulary. Each key word has a linked, mouse-over pop-up definition. This online feature allows for quick and constant reference to the target terms thereby doubly saturating the text with the focal items (Figure 2.27).

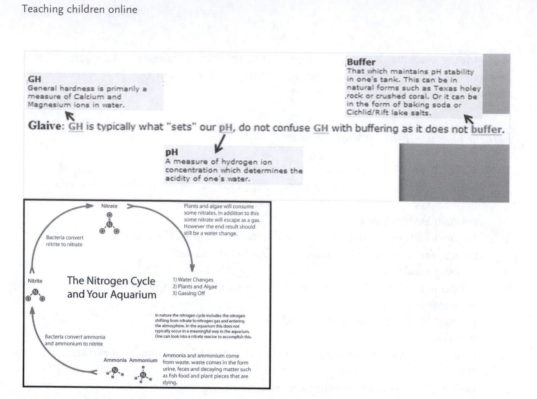

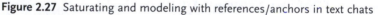

Figure 2.27 Saturating and modeling with references/anchors in text chats

Example: Water chemistry (high school)

T: (*written*) **GH** (*the link to GH says 'General Hardness is primarily a measure of Calcium and Magnesium ions in water'*) *is typically what 'sets' our* **pH** (*the link to pH says 'A measure of hydrogen ion concentration which determines the acidity of one's water'*), *do not confuse* **GH** *with buffering as it does not* **buffer** (*the link to buffer says 'That which maintains pH stability in one's tank. This can be in natural forms such as Texas holey rock or crushed coral. Or it can be in the form of baking soda or Cichlid/Rift lake salts'*). [...] (*displays the chart in the body of the chat*) *There is a diagram of the nitrogen* **cycle** (*the link to cycle says 'A short term for the nitrogen cycle'*).

In addition to the mouse-over feature in text chats, embedded schemas, graphs, diagrams and other images saturated with linguistic models can draw learner attention directly to the focal content.

Eavesdropping on authentic saturations and models

Archives of live chats with book authors, experts on different subjects, publicists, journalists and the like can be a great source for various lesson assignments. Such chats contain a great deal of domain-specific terminology and thereby model its use in authentic and authoritative ways.

The subject of the following chat was *(The Custer Reader)* a book about a boy general who participated in the Civil War. The book's author (Paul Hutton) engages participants in a lively discussion of its contents.

Example: Live chat: Custer's Last Stand *(middle and high school social studies and/or language arts)*

P1:   *(written)* What is your estimate of the number of **Indians** on the battlefield? The article mentions 7,000, but I have heard statistics as low as only 500 of the Indians were warriors capable of fighting.

AU: *(written)* It is impossible to tell, really. We do know that there were far more than 500, based on the **Indians** that surrendered with **Crazy Horse** in the following year. There were certainly several thousand people in the village at **Little Big Horn** and there were certainly enough warriors to take care of the **7th Calvary**.

P2:   *(written)* Was **Crazy Horse** at the battle? Some historians say that when **Custer** was killed, he was still on the way to join the battle.

AU: *(written)* No. **Crazy Horse** was definitely in the fight against **Custer**. **White Bull** and others identified him as being there. But **Crazy Horse** was only one of many **Indian** leaders.

This chat excerpt provides different points of view on specific aspects of the Civil War that remain blank spots in history. The dialogue was saturated with the names of historical figures thus aiding students in appropriating these for their own conversations about this and other related texts and activities.

Text chats with experts in a field can be a great source of discourse saturated with models of the target discourse. The following is an example of a chat with a researcher from the Center for Conservation Biology at the College of William and Mary. She saturated her discourse with many terms from the ornithology field and modeled how to utilize them in broader conversational contexts. Participants in this chat session were eager to pick up these terms and use them in their own postings.

Example: Eagles *(high school)*

Expert: *(written)* During the next 30 day period you will see them gain more **stability** in the nest as they begin to **balance**, build **muscle** and **coordination**. [...] Why don't they walk on feet right away? Other birds do, don't they?

P1:   *(written)* They do not have **muscle**, **balance** or **coordination** until about 30 days old or so. That is one of the differences between **precocial** and **altricial** birds. Those words again

Expert: *(written)* Do the eaglets know who is mom and who is dad? Also who is the dominate partner male of female and who decides where they will nest?

P2:   *(written)* They must learn who their parents are.

Saturating and modeling in text chats: section summary

Text-based chats offer ample opportunities for saturating and modeling target content. As we have seen, specific words and phrases can be rendered salient, reviewable and memorable by doing so. Moreover, in having access to archived chats, both learners and teachers can reflect on and recycle these salient moments and ideas, something not always readily realizable in the live classroom. The real-time nature of chat in conjunction with the text-based anchoring of content makes saturating and modeling particularly effective instructional conversation strategies.

Conclusion

Experienced educators use saturating and modeling in their live classrooms as a matter of course (Cazden & Beck, 2003). They use a range of oral, aural and visual strategies to call learners' attention to what they are in the process of teaching. In online venues, these strategies can be particularly effective in both asynchronous and synchronous environments. In each, instructors and learners have a range of resources they can call upon to amplify their *online saturating* and modeling so that key features of the content under study are pronounced and thus more readily accessible and learnable. As we have seen, modeling for learners how the language of the content area is used in authentic discourse and repeating this given the multiple opportunities for doing so online can work to great pedagogical effect.

End-of-chapter activities

(1) Select one of the illustrations from this chapter. With a partner, analyze the ways in which either saturation or modeling is used. Are there ways you can see these strategies could be used even more effectively given the instructional activity? What about within a different instructional activity? Are these strategies viable? How might you change them?

(2) With a partner, choose a level and content area for which to develop a blog activity. Decide on learning goals and sequencing and develop an example of saturation in the blog activity that includes a teacher and fictional students' voices. Incorporate references within the conversation.

(3) Record a lecture using VoiceThread. Be sure to integrate both saturation and modeling as well as multimodal elements where appropriate. Share your VoiceThread online and see what others have to say about your work.

Further reading

Callow, J. (2008) Show me: Principles for assessing students' visual literacy. *The Reading Teacher* 61 (8), 616–626.

Meskill, C. and Anthony, N. (2005) Foreign language learning with CMC: Forms of instructional discourse in a hybrid Russian class. *System* 33 (1), 89–105.

Spalter, A.M. and Van Dam, A. (2008) Digital visual literacy. *Theory into Practice* 47 (2), 93–101.

Ware, P.D. and Warschauer, M. (2005) Hybrid literacy texts and practices in technology-intensive environments. *International Journal of Educational Research* 43 (7), 432–445.

References

Cazden, C.B. and Beck, S.W. (2003) Classroom discourse. In A.C. Graesser, M.A. Gernsbacher and S.R. Goldman (eds) *Handbook of Discourse Processes* (pp. 165–197). Mahwah, NJ: Lawrence Erlbaum.

Goldenberg, C. (1992) Instructional conversations: Promoting comprehension through discussion. *The Reading Teacher* 46 (4), 316–326.

Meskill, C. and Anthony, N. (2014) Managing synchronous polyfocality in new media/new learning: Online language educators' instructional strategies. *System* 42, 177–188.

Shuell, T. (1988) The role of the student in learning from instruction. *Contemporary Educational Psychology* 13 (3), 276–295.

3

Corralling student learning in online teaching

In this chapter you will learn:

- how the online instructional conversation strategy *corralling* works;

- how corralling works when *Teaching with Voice*, *Teaching with Text* and *Teaching in Real Time*;

- how corralling as an instructional conversation strategy can be undertaken in a range of online environments;

- how corralling can be playful and humorous;

- how each environmental affordance can be optimized to support and amplify these instructional conversation strategies alone and in combination with other affordances.

About corralling

In online teaching, a very effective instructional strategy is to *corral* student learning. This means guiding learners to produce oral, written and/or visual responses that make accurate, articulate and productive use of the target subject area ideas and the specific language that the discipline uses to express those ideas. The analogy 'to corral' or to 'round up' implies positioning and repositioning oneself in response to learners' moves and actions so that one is set in a productive direction toward meeting instructional objectives. In short, it is a verbal means of cornering learners into thinking and communicating in discipline-appropriate ways, thereby demonstrating authentic mastery of content, concepts and the language used to articulate these (Meskill & Anthony, 2005). In this chapter, we illustrate and discuss this powerful oral, written and/or visual strategy in the context of several examples.

Corralling with voice

In a VoiceThread online environment whereby teachers and learners audio-record and then post their messages asynchronously, corralling can mean prompting students to generate responses that reflect both immediate and incidental learning goals. The asynchronous nature of the conversation allows time for thinking through new concepts, consulting resources, deeply considering tasks and assignments and carefully constructing appropriate responses – responses that are aural, public and reviewable by both teachers and classmates. Corralling can be achieved by assigning tasks or asking questions that require students to develop oral responses that include the use of specific terms and then scaffolding students' spoken and written utterances as the conversation develops.

Corralling students into using clear definitions

Example: Triangle scavenger hunt (middle school math)

The explicit use of definitions is something that even young learners should be encouraged to do.

In the following example, a middle school teacher corrals students into using precise mathematical terms they have learned, such as **scalene**, **isosceles**, **acute** or **obtuse**, by asking them to find and define triangles in the series of pictures she included in her voice thread. She then takes on a new persona, feigning ignorance of the subject, thereby corralling the learning of the target language and concepts by taking on the role of a learner herself (Figure 3.1).

T: (*oral*) I gotta tell you that I have absolutely no math ability whatsoever. So as I work through your voice thread, I'm gonna look for a triangle that I can classify based on my very limited knowledge and understanding of math. If I say something wrong,

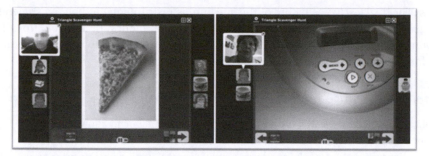

Figure 3.1 Corralling students into using clear definitions in VoiceThread

I'm sure you'll correct me because like I said I'm no expert at this stuff but I'm certainly gonna give it a word.

S1: (*oral*) I realize that this one on this side of the pizza is just a little bit longer than that one, and of course the crust is obviously shorter than both. So I think that this is a **scalene triangle**. It's also making me quite hungry.

S2: (*written*) yummy that looks good. Though it is hard to tell what that is for a triangle because the rounded side at the top, i still think that the 2 angles next to the crust are equal and the point is a acute which makes it a **isosceles triangle**.

T: (*oral*) Hi. I'm looking on this picture and I see this **triangle** right here. It's a printer button I believe. Um... I think this looks like an **equilateral triangle** 'cause it looks to me like all the three sides are equal but it's really interesting when I kinda think about this I wonder why they picked an **equilateral triangle** instead of **isosceles** or **scalene** I mean. What do you think?

S1: (*oral*) I think this is a go button obviously and the **triangle** type can be well anything. It doesn't really matter. **Scalene** would look kind of weird. **Isosceles** would look just like that which would kind of be almost like the same thing but I don't think it's really matter what kind of triangle.

S2: (*written*) I agree with you on the **equilateral** part... but i also think that this **triangle** could be classified as an **acute triangle** because all three side are acute or less than 90 degrees.

In this example, the teacher models the use of the terms in her initial utterance by saturating her discourse with disciplinary terminology (equilateral, isosceles, scalene, etc.). She provides definitions and arranges the task to prompt students to articulate their thinking skills and make authentic use of these terms. Not only does she engage her students in dialogue about triangles, but by carefully shaping her discourse she prompts them to elaborate and refer to different classifications of triangles. Based on real-life examples, the teacher labels the types of triangles in the picture, providing reasons for her choice of definitions and asking her students questions that prompt them to share their own thoughts and ideas. She presents herself as a person who looks, analyzes and discusses her thinking, not as an expert who knows all. She models one way of thinking and provides reasons for her conclusions. She thus corrals her students into thinking, reasoning and articulating. The asynchronous nature of VoiceThread permits additional time that students can use to consult resources: glossaries, textbooks, dictionaries or online sources. The dual text/voice nature of this medium is instrumental in helping students learn and practice new definitions in both oral and written modes. In addition, VoiceThread environments allow students who are reluctant to speak, the option to respond in written/visual form in place of speaking (Meskill & Anthony, 2015).

Example: Distributive property (middle school math)

The following voicethread was created by another math teacher to allow her students practice saying aloud verbal interpretations of focal mathematical symbols. The asynchronous nature of the medium permits careful consideration prior to recording and modifying recordings as needed (Figure 3.2).

S1: (*oral*) On this problem, I see that there are variables on both sides. [...] First, you want to **unlock the parentheses** by using the **distributive property**. [...]

S2: (*oral*) On this problem, you need to use a **distributive property** to **unlock the parentheses**.

S3: (*oral*) OK, for this problem, I would start up by using the **distributive property**. You can see that there are two sides of this **equation**.

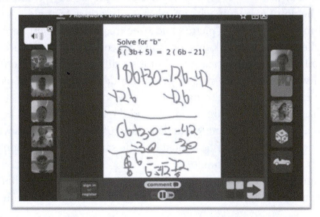

Figure 3.2 Corralling students into using clear definitions in VoiceThread

Using appropriate definitions for corresponding symbols as the goal, this activity was right on target. An outside observer even posted the comment, 'The vocabulary the students are using is wonderful'.

Corralling students into using sources provided

All learners should be capable of gathering and making productive use of information from a variety of sources in order to respond to a learning task. Referring or anchoring to outside sources in *voicethreads* can be facilitated by the multiple opportunities afforded by online venues and the ease with which these can be linked and referenced.

Example: Music genres (elementary school)

In this example, the instructor, whose goal is student mastery of the terms denoting musical genres in their textual, visual and auditory representations, makes systematic reference to different sources. This multimedia aspect makes the characteristics of the targeted musical genres more salient, more memorable. As we can see in this example, the discourse of musical genre identification can be enlivened in many ways through these anchored referents (Figure 3.3).

T: (*oral*) This is my slide show about music genres. Please look at the pictures, click on the **links**, read **Wikipedia articles**, watch the **videos on YouTube**, make comments, and ask questions. **In what ways these music genres are similar and in what ways they are different for each other?**

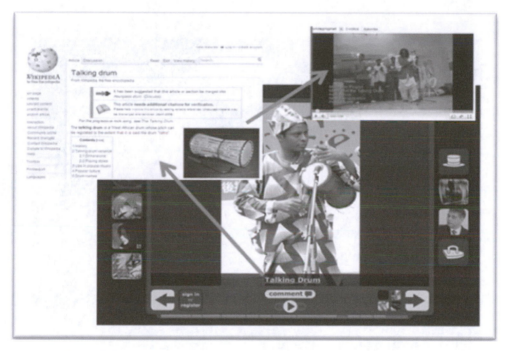

Figure 3.3   Corralling students into using provided sources in VoiceThread

Through the language used in these various visual, textual and auditory anchors, learners are guided to incorporate these terms, constructs and linguistic structures into their evolving disciplinary discourse. To learn about talking drums, students can listen to their instructor and then, referred to the Wikipedia article, explore their subject-specific discourse such as **dimensions** or **playing styles**. In turn, students will not only experience visual and auditory representations of the musical phenomenon, but also enrich their discourse with the names of geographical locations where this particular musical instrument is used: **Nigeria**, **Senegal** and **Northern Ghana**.

Corralling into comparisons and contrasts

In addition to being a highly valued skill in school assessments, the development of student competence in undertaking comparison and contrast clearly encourages deeper understandings and connections. Corralling the development of these complex skills is readily realizable in online teaching.

Example: Interpreting the past (elementary social studies)

In this example, the teacher involves her elementary school students in interpreting the past by making connections and comparisons with the present (Figure 3.4).

T: (*oral and written*) This is **how** the teachers **used to call** the students for school. **How does** your teacher **call** you for class?

Figure 3.4   Corralling students into comparisons and contrasts in VoiceThread

Comparisons and contrasts can be taught in a variety of disciplines using age-appropriate examples. For example, a teacher can use a VoiceThread activity with texts, images and visual recordings for students to compare and contrast (Figure 3.5).

Example: Comparisons (elementary school math)

T: (*oral*) **Compare** the length, weight, and volume of two or more objects by using direct comparison or a nonstandard unit.

Figure 3.5 Corralling students into comparisons and contrasts in VoiceThread

Interdisciplinary corralling

There are interdisciplinary ways to corral students into learning both the content pertaining to a specific discipline along with related subjects as a way to expand their horizons and to enrich their understanding of the world. This we call interdisciplinary corralling.

Example: Geometry (middle school)

The importance of foundational reading skills and the necessity of developing them across the curriculum cannot be overestimated. In the following activity, a middle school teacher corrals students not only into using mathematical terms but also into reading and listening about world famous architecture at the same time. She thereby guides her students to broaden this new knowledge while they develop their reading and listening comprehension skills through links to YouTube videos and other internet sites. The images on the teacher's slide prompt them to read more and learn more about these buildings using the online resources carefully evaluated and made available by their teacher (Figure 3.6).

T: (*oral*) Today we are going to look at geometry as it occurs in our world. These are the photos of some famous buildings: **Parthenon in Greece, Burj Al Arab** in Dubai, **St. Basil Cathedral** in Moscow, Russia, and **Fuji Terebi building in Tokyo, Japan. You can read more about them by clicking on the links provided at the bottom.** How many different **shapes** do you see in these pictures? Do all of these shapes fit into specific categories?

S1:   (*written*) **cone, triangle, hexagon, rectangle, square**

S2:   (*oral*) **Spheres** in the **Fuji Terebi building**.

S3:   (*written*) I see **rectangles** in the **Parthenon** building and circles. I see **ovals** in **Fuji Terebi**. An **oval** is sometimes called an **ellipse**.

S4:   (*oral*) I saw a **triangle** in **Burj Al Arab**.

Figure 3.6 Interdisciplinary corralling in VoiceThread

The asynchronous aspect allows students to take their time reading not only about the subject *per se* but also about related topics. They also practice writing and saying the target terminology in productive and authentic ways.

Structuring tasks for corralling

Structuring tasks is extremely important in making corralling a successful instructional strategy. Attention to details such as clear directions on how to accomplish tasks successfully, the number of required posts, what sources to consult and the length and quality of the products they should produce is critical. The importance of directing learners to use formal, academic language cannot be overemphasized in asynchronous online environments where teachers are not present and students cannot immediately receive coaching and direction.

Example: World art comparison project

The following is an excellent example of a task design with detailed directions provided in both oral and written forms. Channeling information in two modalities achieves the goal of creating a well-structured corralling task. It is never excessive to remind students about the proper use of the language of the content under study. The instructor in the world art comparison project does this frequently and well (Figure 3.7).

Figure 3.7   Task structuring for corralling in VoiceThread

T: (*oral*) Hey there, World Art students! Welcome to your voice thread writing prompt. Now before you start thinking what the assignment directions are I'd like you to spend a couple of minutes exploring the site. You can use the arrow in the corner of your page to click forward and back between the images or you can choose to click on the individual images as you go. Also notice that when you move the mouse over the image, you get a little magnifying glass and you can use that to zoom it and zoom out. Written directions will pop up with each new image page. Also I will tell you little about each image on the page as you go. The directions for your writing assignment are as follows. Pick any two of the following six artifacts we have studied in class and, even though they are from different cultures, times, and places in the world, I want you to discuss how they are similar in at least two ways. Your response must be contained to a single paragraph. Remember to form a strong thesis statement, provide supporting information and details on why the artifacts are alike in at least two ways, and write a conclusion that wraps it all up. **Please remember that this is an academic assignment, not a text message. So keep your writing in Standard English please.** And now for your first image, this is samurai warrior body armor from Japan. This particular uniform you see was mainly for ceremonies. Samurais served and protected the Japanese Emperor. You can find out even more if you refer to your study guide on Japanese art.

T: (*written*) Pick any TWO of the following six artifacts we have studied in class and, even though they are from different cultures, times, and places in the world, discuss how they are similar in at least two ways. Your response must be contained to a single paragraph. Remember to form a strong thesis sentence, provide supporting information and details on why the artifacts are alike in at least two ways, and write a conclusion that wraps it all up. *Remember, this is an academic assignment – not a text message!!* (*oral*) This is a whole Chinese army made of clay. Each figure is life sized and made to look like an individual. They are wearing a traditional soldier's uniform of that time. You can find out even more about this by referring to your study guide on traditional Chinese art.

S1:   (*both oral and written*) In my Introduction to World Art class, I have learned that many different artworks from different cultures are used for the same general purposes. In Japan during the Shogun period, this samurai warrior body armor was used to protect the emperor. It was life sized. In the Chinese culture, a terracotta army was made to protect the emperor in the afterlife. All seven thousand of these figures were also life sized. These two pieces of artwork are very different in many ways including their cultures, yet, they are still used for the same general purpose of protecting the emperor in different aspects of his life.

S2:   (*both oral and written*) Though the Chinese life-sized Terracotta Army and the Japanese Samurai Warrior Body Armor are from different times and civilizations, they have two distinct similarities. Both the Japanese Samurai's and the Chinese Warrior's jobs were to protect the emperor. The other thing the two had in common is that they did not actually perform this job. The Chinese army is made of clay and was placed around a Qin emperor's tomb to protect him in his afterlife. The samurai Body Armor was intricately decorated and only worn for special ceremonies rather than in actual battle. These similarities between the two are unusual because of the time and distance between the creation of them.

It is apparent from the students' responses that this teacher reached her goal. By carefully structuring and explaining the task, she corralled her students into using subject-specific terminology while expressing their ideas.

Example: This is art? (elementary school)

In this example, the teacher has students examine and reflect on pieces of art according to the template: Who made it? What is the title? Why do you like it? What do these pieces have in common? By providing this structure, the teacher corrals students into constructing goal-oriented monologues with these specific purposes in mind (Figure 3.8).

T: (*written*) If you picked one from here, Don't forget to tell me... – Who made it? – What is the title? – WHY do you like it? – What does it have in common with the rest on this slide? Create a category :)

S1:   (*oral*) My favorite one is *House of Parliament: London; Sun Breaking Through the Fog; 1904* by Claude Manet. I think it is gives very distressing feelings but still shows light who is reaching for whom. The texture of the picture looks very rough. It doesn't look very smooth, the surface of the picture... I think the comparison between the three pictures that are on the slide is that they all show the expressions... Look at the goat's face here (*circles the animal's face on the picture*). Their eyes are distressed. They are having a very difficult time with what they are doing. The castle on the top (*circles*) looks like it's distressed. Very much.

S2:   (*written*) The title is *I and the Village* by Marc Chagall. I liked this painting because all of the different colors and the way they bring you into the picture. They are all pretty calming and it doesn't make you think very hard and strain your brain with so many colors.

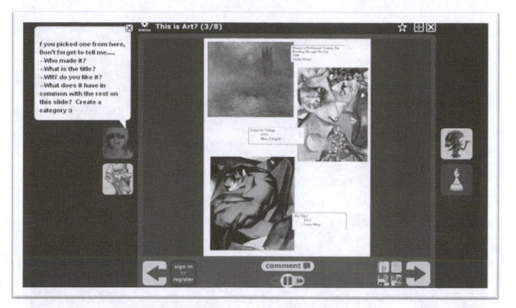

Figure 3.8 Structuring task toolkits

While the task is structured, students are given much freedom in expressing themselves. This is activated by the open-ended question they have to answer: Why do you like this?

Corralling projects in VoiceThread

VoiceThread is an excellent venue for conducting class projects (Wood *et al.*, 2013). Careful planning and structuring of a project is highly important, especially if the project is to be undertaken by elementary school students as in the following example. Besides selecting a topic, a teacher has to evaluate and select sources to be used, arrange roles for the students and equip them with clear directions and resources for them to proceed. VoiceThread, with its capability for uploading images and videos, is a powerful tool for carrying out and presenting class projects as reflected in the following example.

Example: The Great Depression (elementary)

In this example, a fifth-grade teacher assigned a project for her students about the Great Depression based on the book *Poetry for Two Voices*. She sought the help of her school's technology facilitator to help students locate background knowledge about this period in US history (Figure 3.9).

F: (*oral*) When I was searching for web sites for the students to use, I was particularly moved by the photos from that era. I let this project simmer in my mind for few days trying to think of the ways for students the hardship that men, women, and especially children went through during this difficult period in our country's history. I wanted to make this project more meaningful for our students and have them walk

Figure 3.9 Corralling projects in VoiceThread

in the shoes of someone who experienced it firsthand. I found my inspiration in the book *Poetry for Two Voices* by Paul Fleishman. By working with a partner and writing a poem for two voices, serious issues such as the Great Depression could come aligned in a personal and powerful way. Each pair of students can become the people on the photograph they've selected and write about their experiences and emotions from their points of view. It provided the way to personalize these events to help students and even you, the audience, better understand the historical context.

T: (*oral*) Writing a poem from the perspective of a person who lived through the Depression required my students to think about the struggle those people went through in a personal way. The photographs used in class sparked wonderful discussions. Students used a variety of print and online resources to generate **meaningful words and phrases** to describe their photographs. Students analyzed the photographs using both **objective and subjective terms**.

Ss: (*oral*) There is just not enough. I feel ashamed that I cannot afford food for my children. My daddy left us to go out to find work. I feel lost. I have no hope. My brother suffers from malnutrition. The pain is overwhelming. We have very little. I only have one rag doll. My children are thinner than they should be. Disaster! Chaos... The bank took our home away. A new house is only made of cardboard and woods from the dumpsters. I only had a piece of bread for lunch. I rely on plants to feed my family. We had to give our dog away 'cause we couldn't pay for his food. There is just not enough. Jobs. Food. Water. Colds. Money. Rain. Time. There is just not enough. Hope.

This is an outstanding example of constructive and thought-provoking ways to develop projects with VoiceThread. The students were given precise instructions and the freedom to create their own poems on the subject, thereby engaging in a creative process that was meaningful for them while prompting them to use and connect both their active and passive vocabulary.

Student projects in VoiceThread can be shaped in part by collaborating classmates whose questions corral presenters into deeper thinking on the subject and into looking up answers when necessary (Brunvand & Byrd, 2011). In the following example, the teacher instructed her students to ask the presenter questions as a means of corralling. This clearly made it even more informative and interesting for the audience.

Example: Catfish (elementary school science)

S1: (*oral*) First, catfish have eggs. Catfish carry the eggs in their mouth.

S2: (*oral*) **Why do they keep eggs in their mouths?**

S3: (*oral*) **How many eggs do their hold in their mouths and how small are they?** Because I think the smaller they are, the more are there.

S1: (*oral*) They hold eggs in their mouths to make sure they stay safe. They can have up to 2,000 and up to 100,000. They are smaller than a centimeter, they are way smaller like 1/8 of a centimeter. Isn't that interesting? And they are the same size no matter what.

Corralling with voice: section summary

Where the bulk of online instruction is text based, the addition of the voices of the instructor, classmates and outside experts can clearly enhance the quality of interaction with course materials. As we have seen in the preceding examples, when a skilled instructor corrals learning via voice, learners are guided to more fully and actively engage the subject matter at hand.

Corralling with text

As we have seen in oral asynchronous environments, corralling is especially facilitated by the element of time: time for students to compose their posts, time for instructors to detect and design corralling strategies in response to teachable moments and time for all to consider and reflect on instructional conversations overall. The asynchronous and written nature of discussion forums (discussion forums, threads, boards and blogs) allows for corralling to be carefully crafted by a teacher and carefully carried out by students. Moreover, the technical features of many existing programs make multilevel corralling in discussion forums very effective. Videos discussing the situation from different angles, links to articles analyzing opposing views and well thought-through and clearly articulated teacher questions and expectations guide students into thinking critically and thoroughly and in turn expressing their ideas at a high level. Corralling is an effective instructional strategy for getting learners back on track by attending to and employing the targeted discourse of the moment in ways that assist them in incorporating those subject-specific terms into their developing repertoire. As we have discussed, employing this kind of redirecting strategy as part of the natural stream of communication is an effective method for teaching learners to notice, attend to, comprehend and discuss new concepts productively.

Corralling students into using subject-specific vocabulary

Blogs are an excellent way to engage students in using discipline-specific discourse. Starter questions or prompts in blogs can be open-ended to encourage students to use as much vocabulary from the field as possible in meaningful communication.

Example: The periodic table (middle school chemistry)

T: (*written*) What do you already know about the Periodic Table and the information it provides?

S1:   (*written*) Things I know about the periodic table is that there are **elements**, and the table is split up into **sublevels** which helps us identify the number of levels it has.

S2:   (*written*) There is a set of **gases**, **solids**, and **liquids**.

S3:   (*written*) The periodic table is arranged in **groups** and **periods** so that **elements** with similar **characteristics** are near each other (in groups and periods). **Elements** on the periodic table can bond **ionically** and **covalently** to form **compounds**.

S4:   (*written*) I know that the periodic table organizes the **elements**. I know that it separates them into **gases**, **liquids**, and **solids** and they are also split into **energy levels** and **sublevels**.

This kind of blog activity is an excellent way to refresh students' memories before starting a new topic that builds on the previous one. It is an excellent method for orienting learners to specific disciplinary discourse contexts.

Structuring tasks

Example: The case of Genie (high school psychology)

In this example, the teacher's goal is to help students conceptualize the ethical versus unethical treatment of patients. She corrals students into using specific terms by designing the task around a series of videos centered on the story of Genie, the girl who lived isolated in her room until she was ten years old. A series of questions corralled students into active, well-established reasoning and the consideration of different points of view. The videos provide the discipline-specific terminology for students to use in their responses. The teacher's questions are displayed on the slide corralling them into desired directions (Figure 3.10).

Student responses reveal productive use of targeted terms: case studies, psychological experiments, ethics, ethical standards, long-term harm, confidentiality, valid/invalid arguments, generalization, scientific methods and the like. The teacher structured student answers by prompting them to build their answers through reasoning and deep

Figure 3.10 Task design for corralling in discussion boards

knowledge of the situation. This helped learners to compose mature, carefully crafted posts. The teacher clearly stated her expectations and what she would and would not welcome as responses. Students responded accordingly.

T: (*written*) Was the lawsuit filed by Genie's mother justified? Weigh in on your opinion, here, but be sure to **substantiate your response**. This should **not be just a gut reaction**, but a **well thought out explanation**.

S1:   (*written*) Genie's mother was **ethically** right, but morally wrong. It was **unethical** of the psychologists to study Genie without **informed consent** and consent from her parents since Genie would not understand the question. And after awhile the psychologists were accused of having no **scientific purpose** for studying Genie. They allegedly kept giving her tests just to give them to her. For these reasons the lawsuit was justified. The lawsuit was morally wrong though. Genie's mother was morally wrong filing this lawsuit. She had no right to say the psychologists were in wrongdoing when she was the one who let the abuse happen in her house and didn't try to help her daughter.

S2:   (*written*) I watched the clip and saw/heard no mention of a lawsuit? If there actually was a lawsuit filed, which I'm assuming there was, its legitimacy would be entirely dependent upon which 'mother' filed it. If it was her nearly blind, negligent, biological mother, the lawsuit would have no grounds, as the **treatment** Genie received as a **test-subject**, no matter how 'inhumane' she [the mother] viewed it as, was infinitely better than what she received at her original home. Additionally, the old mother presumably lacked all custody rights, so she would have no grounds upon which to sue. If it was a lawsuit filed by her new, foster-mother Jean Butler (?), I could see the case as having some **legitimacy**, as all **testing**, in order to **comply** with **ethical testing standards**, would have to go through the guardians of the child involved. In addition, another **stipulation of the ethical standards** is the ability to **withdraw** from said **experimentation** at any point in time. If the new mother felt that the testing was a **detriment** or **hindrance** to either Genie or their family as a whole, she'd reserve the right to remove the child from **the testing environment**, even though it would be adverse to the acquisition of scientific knowledge and would be hypocritical and backhanded, as she was, at one point, a tester on Genie.

The combination of an online learning medium that allows for the time needed to read, think and construct intelligent, on-target responses, along with a carefully crafted instructional task supported by teacher scaffolding makes this an excellent example of how corralling can be used to achieve instructional goals, especially those that include active student articulation of new concepts using discipline-appropriate language. Students can watch the videos several times and spend a substantial amount of time developing responses that incorporate domain-specific vocabulary.

Corralling and the task toolkit

Keeping students focused on what is to be learned, especially in asynchronous modes when a teacher is not always available for immediate guidance, is an essential priority in online teaching (Kim & Bonk, 2010). Structuring directions can be done through the focal information in the *task toolkit* – that constant onscreen text box to which students can refer throughout as they record, review and re-record their posts. The task toolkit is a set of elements that learners may need to refer to and make use of during a task. An advantage of online instruction in this regard is that these toolkits can be collected and managed in a class task repository and referred to as needed and/or used in assessments. This form of self-control and self-assessment can help students become accustomed to structured thinking. It is a particularly attractive aspect of the oral asynchronous mode where students can easily refer to the task toolkit in order to better structure and articulate their responses. This kind of structural corralling is one productive way of implementing this instructional conversation strategy.

Corralling with the task toolkit

Example: Next time take the train

In this instance, a teacher asks students to integrate three aspects of a picture into their posts. A detailed explanation of the three aspects resides in the toolkit. In this way, this teacher corrals her students' thinking in a particular direction. The *task toolkit* corrals students into employing proper development and organization. It is a constant reminder of requirements on the screen (Figure 3.11).

T: (*written*) There are **three things** we could talk about here – **content, context**, and **form**. By **content** I mean what's happening in this image, by **context** I mean the historical moment this was made in – 1932 and how that informs our understanding of this image. By **form**, I mean how the image looks – how the forms are arranged, the composition, light and dark, space, texture, contrast, shapes, etc. So, feel free to comment on one of those three issues – just state first which one you are addressing. Also, as much as possible I would like to focus on FORM – since that is hardest, and it is also, I think, where works of art derive most of their power.

S: (*written*) **Content** wise, the two men are walking away from something. Perhaps they are moving their lives somewhere else to make a better living for themselves. I think we should also take notice that one is taller than the other and that Lange may have been trying to capture an older person and a younger one (father and son; big brother

Figure 3.11   Corralling into structured thinking in discussion boards

and younger brother). In terms of **context**, this area seems to be rural due to the dirt road and farm lands and during the Great Depression time, farms suffered a 40–60% crop profit. Perhaps these men were farmers and this is the reason they are moving. It is rather ironic for the billboard to be advertising something that many during that time could not afford. These men are obviously not as relaxed as train riders but this is because they could not afford to take a train. The **form** is very interesting. Although we are not to talk about colors, I think it is clear that there is a obvious dark area surrounding the men (i.e. the road, the sky above them and the farmlands). However, the sky ahead of them is illuminous and rays of sunshine (white lines) are breaking up the dark skies. Lastly, I would like to call attention to the dark line that is running parallel to the men and the road. Lange clearly was dividing the men from the railroad. The dark line was to show that these men did not have the capital to 'relax'. This little visual sends a powerful message that these males did not have the option because of their financial situation.

The development and organization of ideas in this written asynchronous activity are guided by a skillful teacher. She employs precise terms, modeling these and equipping students with brief definitions. She thereby sets clear expectations for students' responses.

Playful corralling

Example: Why do people hate?

Experienced teachers can engage students through playfulness. In this example, the teacher started a discussion about hatred. The task was designed as a series of quotes about hate supplemented with provocative questions aimed at analyzing different aspects of hatred: Is hate really taught? Do kids learn hate from their parents? What is the connection between hatred and fear? Are there direct connections between hatred and understanding? What steps should we take to try to end hatred in our world? The following authors were cited: 'In time we hate that which we often fear' (Shakespeare); 'I think that hate is a thing, a feeling, that can only exist where there is no understanding' (Tennessee Williams). The teacher provides a drawing depicting two men, one of whom is saying 'I hate this guy'. This switch from a 'serious' conversation about 'hate' in the sphere of everyday life had a drastic effect on the discussion participants, showing them how the concept of hate penetrates our daily lives and that it is actually not an abstract notion but a real one. In doing so, the teacher directed the participants to consider hatred from fresh though familiar perspectives (Figure 3.12).

Figure 3.12 Playful corralling in discussion boards

S1:   (*written*) This image brings up an interesting thought. By using a word too much, **does it lose its meaning? Webster defines** hate, 'n. a strong dislike v. to have a strong feeling of disgust for'. By casually using hate in our everyday conversations, **does the power of this word get lost?**

S2:   (*written*) I believe so, Student 1. We use the word hate when we are even the slightest bit upset and sometimes just to be funny. The word 'hate' should be used only to represent absolute disgust. We overuse this word so much that when we actually mean it, it may not seem that way. Look in the picture, it doesn't look like the person on the right really means what he is saying, but the person on the left seems offended anyway. Then the person on the left might believe that the person on the right really hates him and react accordingly.

S3:   (*written*) I think that if people use the word hate every day, then yes it will lose its meaning. People will begin to think that you hate everything in life. Even if you don't hate everything, then you sure make it look like it. Do you think that people mean to use the word hate on an everyday basis, and if so **what reason do they have to use it?** All this just makes it all the harder to understand and deal with true hate.

In this example, text-based discussions, although employing formal written modes of communication, can turn colloquial. This activity is an excellent example of a well-crafted corralling task that not only provokes answers but also stimulates questions and prompts using outside sources.

Persistent corralling

Corralling as an instructional conversation strategy is not only important at the beginning of an activity: designing the task, developing a task toolkit and setting up its components. It is also crucial throughout an instructional activity as a way to guide student learning.

Example: European influence on the American revolution (high school history)

Here, the teacher posted a question on the slide: 'What role did European rivalries and alliances play in the American Revolutionary War?' On the next slide, he suggests 'Read through the Key Question, Need to Know and Dilemma to figure out what type of influence European nations had on the American Revolution'. He also provides a link to the American History website that contains all the documents required for the task. By asking questions, making clarifying remarks and providing explanations, he both corralled and scaffolded his students, thereby helping them form well-founded arguments (Figure 3.13).

Figure 3.13   Persistent corralling

T: (*written*) Based on the information you gathered from ABC Clio, post two comments. One original thought, and one response to a classmate.

S1:   (*written*) If France had not of intervened in the American revolution and helped the colonies then colonial independence would have been very remote to obtain.

S2:   (*written*) If the colonists didn't have the French as an ally they would not have gained the strength that they did.

S3:   (*written*) After reading the info on ABC-clio, I've learned that the Franco-American Alliance, signed on February 6, 1778, was a MAJOR turning point in the war.

S4: (*written*) I wonder if more countries would have gotten involved if they had the chance?

T: (*written*) Student 2, countries don't have friends, only interests. **Can we really blame any European nation?**

S5: (*written*) If the foreign countries had not stepped in to help the colonies, they wouldn't have had a very good chance at gaining independence.

S6: (*written*) One of the negative effects was the Revolution was a continuation of the rivalry between European powers.

T: (*written*) **Why hasn't anyone mentioned the fact that the French took forever to officially back the colonists?** Waiting until after their victory at Saratoga to fledge full support.

S7: (*written*) If the French hadn't contributed to the American side of the war, the colonists may have not won the war. If they had just continued the way they were fighting without help, the end result would have been much different.

S8: (*written*) Spain and France both got involved in the American Revolution for their own reasons.

S9: (*written*) Doesn't the whole war stem back to foreign involvement? If you take away the enlightenment ideas that came from other European countries, it is entirely possible that the war would never have occurred, or at the very least been postponed for quite some time. Without the enlightenment, ideas of the government being there for the people, not over the people, may have taken much longer to arise. Therefore, outside countries were involved before the war even began.

T: (*written*) Student 9, of course it all evolved from European involvement. **But ideas don't cause wars, right?**

The teacher in this example persistently corralled his students into productive thinking and disciplinarily appropriate use of terminology.

Corralling using clues

An asynchronous environment provides a unique opportunity for students to follow teachers' clues and to figure out correct answers. They can also arrive at answers by manipulating different *digital learning objects* such as 3D simulations, tables, graphs or formulas. This nicely develops students' contemporary, digital research skills (Figure 3.14).

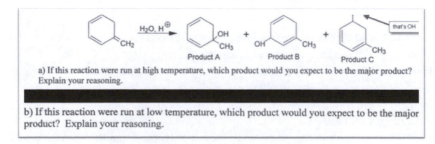

Figure 3.14 Corralling using clues

Example: Organic problem (high school chemistry)

S: (*written*) I have difficulties solving these problems (*refers to the image in Figure 3.14*).

T: (*written*) **Clue**: conjugated compounds (A and C) are thermodynamically more stable. **Look** at the reactivity of an intermediate carbocation and **see** how it will react with nucleophile: water

T: (*written*) **Useful links**:
       http://www.mhhe.com/physsci/chemistry/carey/student/olc/ch04nucle.html

       http://pubs.acs.org/doi/abs/10.1021/ja00365a081
       and thesis:
       http://wvuscholar.wvu.edu:8881//exlibris/dtl/d3_1/apache_media/
       L2V4bGlicmlzL2R0bC9kM18xL2FwYWNoZV9tZWRpYS8yMDYyNQ

Corralling in discussion forums: student projects

Discussion forums are a great venue for students to present their projects and presentations. These can be complemented with follow-up activities in the form of discussion threads around projects and presentations.

Example: Give your classmates feedback – blog entry (middle school chemistry)

The teacher designed and precisely described the structure of this activity and also modeled the types of feedback he expected from his students. Students, following the teacher's lead, kept to the structure of the designed task and provided each other with feedback in just the ways the teacher had modeled. The following is an excellent example of an exchange around pair and group projects.

T: (*written*) Give your classmates **two pieces of warm feedback** and **two pieces of cool feedback** after you explore their project (read their website, complete their webquest, listen to their podcast, etc.).
        Your post should be in **this format**:
        List the names of the group members you are reviewing, their project format (web-site, movie, etc.).
              List your names.
              Two pieces of warm feedback. This feedback should be specific, and phrased like **'I liked that you...'**
              Two pieces of cool feedback. This should also be specific, and should be phrased like **'For improvement, I would suggest...'** Be **polite** and **constructive**.

Ss 4/5: (*written*) Student 1, Student 2, Student 3 – website. Reviewers: Student 4, Student 5. Warm: **We liked that** you included a lot of great information and went in depth on even more complicated topics like the superstring theory. Impressive! Good job making it conversational as well as informative. Cool: **Maybe you could** include a few more pictures/diagrams, and more on the current atomic model. Overall, really great job though.

Ss 9/10:   (*written*) Student 6, Student 7, Student 8
           WEBQUEST
           Student 9, Student 10
           Warm: **We liked** the student evaluation – the categories were very fair. Also, the powerpoint was well done, a good idea, and very informative.
           Cool: **For improvement, we would suggest** more images because it makes it more visually appealing. Second – we thought the process page could have been more organized.
           Excellent job!

This blog-based feedback exchange about group projects is well structured and organized, making it an excellent teaching/learning tool.

Corralling with text: section summary

Asynchronous text-based forms of corralling are particularly productive as regards *time* and students' and teachers' consequent opportunities to examine, reflect and compose. The metaphor of actively and aggressively guiding (corralling) someone to understand and articulate constitutes a key instructional conversation strategy in online educational processes.

Corralling in audio/video conferencing

Synchronous online venues are obviously constrained by the element of time. Moreover, when novice teachers begin teaching via audio/video conferencing in online environments such as the Wimba Classroom, Blackboard Collaborate, Adobe Connect, WebEx or other audiographic applications, many experience frustration and become intimidated by certain features of the medium: lack of eye contact, gestures, facial expressions and other real-time reactions we experience in face-to-face interactions. It takes time and patience to become comfortable communicating in such venues. However, affordances such as easy, immediate access to and availability of various online resources, the use of video and text-based chat or instant messaging when cleverly integrated can mediate the more awkward aspects. A key element is to provide effective cues and guidance so that learners can both comprehend and produce the discourse that the instructor intends. A strategy that helps focus on instructional objectives is corralling.

In audio/video conferencing, corralling means prompting students to use subject-specific language in meaningful exchanges with the instructor and classmates as a means of both learning and assessment. The dual text+voice nature means there is opportunity for every student to participate in the task at hand and generate thoughtful responses. Corralling can be achieved by asking questions or assigning tasks that require students to converse using specific terms and then, in turn, scaffolding students' spoken and written utterances to achieve this goal. Like in asynchronous environments, in synchronous online environments instructors and students can share and make use of links to various sources to enhance and strengthen the power of corralling.

Corralling can be performed in ways similar to what occurs in face-to-face classrooms with a teacher asking questions and eliciting answers that require appropriate use of subject-specific vocabulary. The difference is that most teachers using audio/video conferencing prefer that students type the answers into the chat areas to save time. As mentioned earlier, this also allows shy students who are reluctant to speak, to participate as well. This is reflected in the following example.

Example: Environmental science (middle school)

T: (*oral*) OK, that's how it's going to work. All the questions will be on the screen, and if you know the answer, type it into this little chat section of the main room. The first person to type a correct answer will get extra points. Ready?
      First question. What is the **natural resource** being **drilled** for when we are talking about the **Marcellus Shale**? What kind of natural resource?

S1:   (*written*) **oil**

S2:   (*written*) **oil**

S3:   (*written*) **oil**

T: (*oral*) **Oil**? No. Good guess, the three of you. No, they are not **drilling** for **oil**. What are they...

S4:   (*written*) **natural gas**

S3:   (*written*) **gas**

T: (*oral*) Bing-bing-bing! Student 4 got it! They are **drilling** for **gas**.

S1:   (*written*) wayy to go student 4

S1:   (*written*) lol

T: (*oral*) Next item. What type of **shale** is it? Does anybody remember the name of that **shale**?

S3:   (*written*) **shale**

T: (*oral*) Yeah. But you have to talk about the specific texture, Student 1. What is the name of the **shale**?

S2:   (*written*) **quartz**?

S1:   (*written*) **marcellus**?

T: (*oral*) You got it, Student 1! **Marcellus**. Very good.

Example: Japanese language and culture

In this example, the teacher engages students in a synchronous text-based discussion in the chat area in which they readily use the terms from her model utterances. Thus, they demonstrate mastery of their knowledge of the subject and its specific disciplinary language. This is accomplished in a playful manner. In addition, the instructor uses a web camera to create a sense of a live teacher being present. She also includes personal information to make the communication more personable (Figure 3.15).

Figure 3.15   Corralling in audio/video conferencing

T: (*oral*) (*previously talked about* **aikido**) Let me move on to **origami**. (*pause*) Yes, that's me several years ago.

S1:   (*written*) Is it similar to **karate**? They are sure dressed the same.

S2:   (*written*) I used to take **tae-kwon-do**.

S3:   (*written*) look what I found http://aikido.com/ he was the founder

S4:   (*written*) human **origami**

S5:   (*written*) o m g... look at the anger on her face... she's like a skilled fighter

Corralling using clues

Teachers can use the interactive features of many audio/video conferencing applications that come supplied with chat areas into which URLs to various online sources can be typed or copied and pasted, allowing teachers to easily corral students into applying and training research skills appropriate for their age (Figure 3.16).

Example: World history (middle school social studies)

T: (*orally*) Who founded the fascist party? Remember, this is **Italy**. Do you remember any other leaders of Italy? (*pause*) And who was the gentleman who founded the **fascist party**? (*pastes the following URL in the chat area* http://www.history.com) You know how to make a search by keywords, right?

S: (*written*) **Mussolini**

This example demonstrates that students can be prompted to conduct a basic search using key words from a relevant online source, as they were taught, and quickly take the initiative to find relevant information.

Corralling by quizzing

Corralling can be done through online quizzes and tests. Students can be coached and guided to information and resources that can assist them in their work via, for example, scaffolds typed into the chat box, URL link or an application sharing feature allowing for sharing the information from one's own desktop.

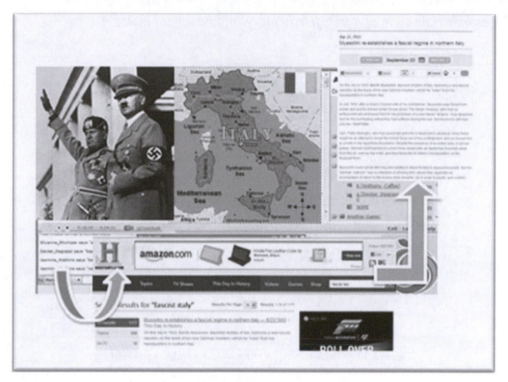

Figure 3.16   Corralling using clues in audio/video conferencing

Example: Energy (middle school earth science)

In this example, a teacher corrals students into writing by offering them an online quiz that she opened on her desktop from http://www.eia.gov/kids/energy.cfm?page=quiz and shared with her students.

T: (*oral*) OK, guys, we'll do it one at a time. OK, the first one. **Coal**, **petroleum**, **natural gas**, and **propane** are **fossil fuels**. They are called **fossil fuels** because: ... – you just put the word down.

S1:   (*oral*) They are called **fossil fuels** because they are burned to **release energy** and they cause **air pollution**.

T: (*oral*) Hmmm... Any other answers?

S2:   (*oral*) They are called **fossil fuels** because they were formed from the buried **remains of plants and** tiny **animals** that lived hundreds of millions of years ago.

The built-in quiz functionality of many audio/video conferencing programs supports corralling via quizzes, something that certainly saves classroom time and provides opportunities for immediate feedback. The following example demonstrates how the teacher corrals his students into using targeted biological terminology by giving them a quick short-answer quiz at the end of his mini-lecture to ensure that all students were attending and now know how to utilize terminology.

Example: Life cycle of a frog (elementary-middle school biology)

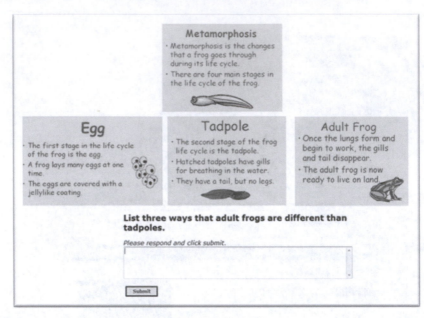

Figure 3.17 Corralling by quizzing in audio/video conferencing

Corralling by assigning group work

Example: Credit card debt (middle school economics)

Some contemporary audio/video conferencing programs are equipped with functions such as arranging breakout rooms. These rooms can be populated with groups of students or pairs who have an assignment they have to complete and then report back to the class. The following is an example from an economics class. The teacher assigned students into small groups, giving each group an assignment to come up with an elaborated answer to one of the following questions: What are the most common causes of credit card debt? What are the alarming consequences? (Figure 3.18)

This type of activity corrals students into both listening to target vocabulary and actively producing appropriate utterances. The following are students' remarks after they worked in small groups in breakout rooms and later came back to the main room to share their brief reports.

S1: (*oral*) We think that not all people who rack up **credit card debts** live out of their **financial limits**, spending irresponsibly, although living beyond one's earnings can be a cause of **credit card debt**. Buying a $1,500 LCD TV set when there is actually no cash for that is foolish.

S2: (*oral*) As Student 1 just said, some people are simply irresponsible and immature living beyond of what they earn monthly but there are some other causes of **financial problems**. Some emergency situations such as unexpected medical bills or divorce can result in **credit card debts**.

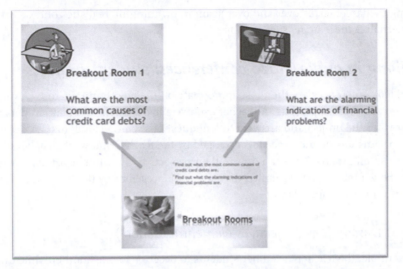

Figure 3.18 Corralling by assigning breakout rooms in audio/video conferencing

S3:   (*written*) you should keep an eye on your wife's **bank account** :))))

S4:   (*oral*) If you get fired all of a sudden from a job that provides an **income** or a large portion of an **income**, that can be also lead to your **credit card debt**. Also, some people are not able to **manage** properly their **budgets** and **calculate** their **expenses** accurately.

S3:   (*written*) i'm so taking math classes!

Students can also be assigned to work in small groups to conduct discussions, develop presentations or work on tasks together. Modern audio/video conferencing technologies allow for such meetings in real time outside the virtual classroom.

Example: Polarity (high school chemistry)

S1:   (*oral*) I have a question. Perhaps it's kinda silly but I wonder if **ozone** is **polar**. I know that it does not have **polar bonds** but I know **oxygen** is **paramagnetic**. It does have **unpaired electrons** and thus is attracted to a **magnetic field**. Also, I know **ozone** has a bent 120 degree shape – which is usually **polar**. Any ideas?

S2:   (*oral*) I had always thought that **polarity** was caused by differing **electronegativities** of the **atoms** involved in a **bond**. If you have two **atoms** of the same **element bonded** to each other, they both have the same **electronegativity** so they would have to be **non-polar**. Is that correct?

S3:   (*oral*) I'd say so. The way I understand it, you need differing **electronegativity** to be **polar**, and if it's a big difference, the bond is no longer **covalent** but **ionic**.

In this example, students assigned to work together on a chemistry problem became engaged in rich conversation filled with chemistry terms and constructs. Such an activity can be conducted on a regular basis while corralling students into extending their discussions while maintaining consistent focus on the target terms and concepts.

Repeating the target terms over and over again in meaningful, realistic contexts can help them internalize these items successfully.

Corralling in audio/video conferences: student projects

Audio/video conferences are the most appropriate online environments for working on and presenting student projects. A teacher can use a live session to explain in detail the procedures for the project and answer student questions. Online students can get together in virtual rooms during the time slots arranged by the teacher and work collaboratively in pairs or in small groups. They can upload their projects to the whiteboard, type, write or draw on the whiteboard or, if granted the status of a presenter by the teacher, share their projects from their own desktops.

Example: Descriptions (adjectives elementary school)

In this example, the teacher asked her students to describe to one another while drawing pictures of each other on the whiteboard using different colors. The goal was to corral her students into using as many descriptive adjectives as possible (Figure 3.19).

Figure 3.19   Corralling student mini-projects in audio/video conferencing

S1:   (*draws a pictures*) (*oral*) This is my friend Amanda. She is 6. She has **blue** eyes and **long blonde** hair. She is **smiley** and **happy**.

S2:   (*draws a picture*) (*oral*) This is Jessica. She is 6 too. She's got **big brown** eyes and **short dark curly** hair. She likes to laugh and play.

Example: Poster presentations

In this example, the teacher conducts a 12-minute live session that is recorded to explain to students the project requirements and provide visual examples. He provided a poster checklist and an example of a student poster project from https://voicethread.com/share/1008104/ (Figure 3.20).

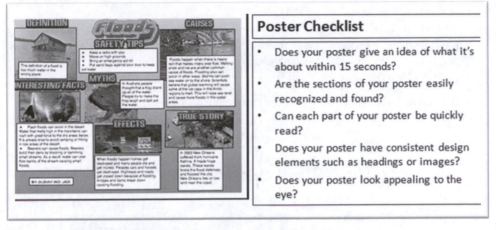

Figure 3.20   Corralling student projects in audio/video conferencing

T: (*oral*) This is an example of a poster presentation addressing all the questions in the poster checklist on the right. As you can see, it orients the audience to the topic in less than several seconds. The poster has several sections that can be easily found and read. Definition, Interesting Facts, Safety Tips, Myths, Effects, Causes, and an example story.

Example: Health project (seventh grade)

In this example, the student gives a presentation while other students, using the chat feature of an audio conferencing program, type in their questions that the student presenter can answer separately or as a part of her presentation. This actually helps students better shape their presentations (Figure 3.21).

S1:   (*using a web feature and an application sharing feature of the program, shows the Mayo Clinic's website and images from the BNN hospital website*) (*oral*) My presentation is about Dengue Fever. It's a dangerous **disease**. It has many **symptoms** of a flu

Figure 3.21   Corralling student projects in audio/video conferencing

infection but it's actually caused by a **virus**. Dengue Fever is carried by mosquitoes when they bite you. Dengue Fever gives people **skin rash**, **muscle and joint pain**, **headaches**, and a very **high fever**.

S2: (*written*) Can you **catch** it in the US?

S3: (*written*) Is there any **cure** like **vaccines**?

S1: (*oral*) Dengue Fever is common in Asia and the Pacific Islands. There is no **vaccines** yet. If you get it, you have to **drink plenty** of water to get it out of your body.

S4: (*written*) How high the **fever** can be?

Projects in audio/video conferences can be carried out in a variety of ways. Adding videos with webcams can evoke the powerful effect of live presence (Figure 3.22).

Figure 3.22   Corralling student projects in audio/video conferencing

Example: Little House in the Big Woods *(elementary school language arts)*

S1: (*oral with video*) I think we start any letter with saying 'hello' first. I think...

S2: (*oral*) Or you say 'dear'...

S3: (*oral*) How about 'Hello Laura'?

S2: (*oral*) Do we want to say how much we like the book?

S1: (*oral*) I guess so.

S3: (*oral*) Who will type? I can type actually. I do it pretty quick.

S1: (*oral*) OK.

S2: (*oral*) Yeah...

S3: (*written*) Dear Laura, We like your book very much.

Providing links to different supporting sources can make the presentation of a project in an audio/video conference format more vivid and have a stronger impact on the audience.

Corralling in audio/video conferencing: section summary

While certainly more challenging than in asynchronous venues, corralling in live audio/video conferencing can guide learner attention and production in a fast-paced, minds-on way. Through questions, cues and leading statements, online instructors can push learners into up-close encounters with new and developing knowledge.

Corralling in text chats

To review, online corralling entails conversational moves that require responses on the part of the learner whereby the target content gets appropriated and, in turn, articulated. The target verbal elements are made clear through the development of the task and its task toolkit so that both the instructor and learners have this focal information continually at hand (on the screen). It is an instructional conversation strategy that succeeds in redirecting learner conversation to a targeted aspect of the target content. Due to the fast pace of chat environments, opportunities to corral students, while more difficult to determine than in asynchronous environments, abound as more real-time spontaneity tends to mean less well focused and developed posts and thus an abundance of rich teachable moments.

Example: Osmosis (high school biology)

http://www.citruscollege.edu/lc/archive/biology/Pages/Chat-Osmosis.aspx

Chat activities can be used productively for one-on-one tutoring during virtual office hours. In this case, the chat does not become confusing due to too many participating voices. The written nature of the chat allows teachers to engage learners in step-by-step problem-solving. They can easily refer to the previous steps to re-read and re-think. In the following example, the teacher corrals a student into answering his own question by guiding his thinking with a series of guiding questions.

S: (*written*) On your chapter note you asked the study question as to why drinking salt-water will dehydrate a person even more. Could you answer the question as to why saltwater dehydrates a person? Can you also briefly explain why saline is used in IVs to hydrate patients.

T: (*written*) **Do you know the terms** hypotonic, hypertonic, and isotonic?

S: Y es, I have an understanding of this.

T: (*written*) **Do you know what happens** if you put red blood cells in a hypertonic solution?

S: (*written*) I believe the cell will rapidly fill with water. It moves from a high concentration to an area of low concentration. This could cause cell damage if to rapid.

T: (*written*) Water always move from hypotonic (high water concentration and low solute conc.) to hypertonic (low water concentration and high solute conc.) solution. If red blood cells (RBC) are placed in hypertonic environment, the water will move from RBC to hypertonic solution.

S: (*written*) Thus dehydrating the cell rapidly?

T: (*written*) Very good. Now, **what happens when** you put RBCs in the hypotonic solution?

S: (*written*) The water will flow into the cell across the membrane, perhaps rapidly.

T: (*written*) Very good and cause the cell to burst, since animal cells have no cell wall like plant cells. This process is called hemolysis. Now **what happens when** you put RBCs in an isotonic solution?

S: (*written*) Is the saline solution used medically a balanced solution thus causing an isotonic condition?

T: (*written*) Yes. Saline is iosotonic to our body fluid.

S: (*written*) The cell will absorb the water it needs but will not absorb to rapidly as to cause burting.

T: (*written*) Since it is iosotonic, same amount of water will go in and out of the cell.

This chat activity was productive in that the teacher did not provide ready answers but, by instructionally conversing with the student, corralled him in the right direction and the use of subject-specific terminology.

Structuring task in chat

Because text-based chat is an extremely dynamic environment, its use as an instructional tool has to be well structured and organized. One of the productive settings where this tool can be used effectively is a live chat with the author of a book. This activity is something that both in-class and online students can take advantage of. While students should always come to a chat prepared with questions and comments well formulated, the spontaneous nature of this medium can provoke discussions that are in some ways similar to face-to-face conversations. In such chats, students engage in dialogue not only with an author but with other participants as well, exchanging ideas, practicing the use of known subject-specific vocabulary, being exposed to new models of academic discourse and having an opportunity to communicate with diverse partners.

Example: Live author chat on book talk (philosophy)

http://www.booktalk.org/transcripts.html

http://www.booktalk.org/chat-transcript-with-author-todd-riniolo-september-24-2009-at-9-00-pm-eastern-t7103.html

The following is an excerpt from a chat with Todd C. Riniolo, the author of *When Good Thinking Goes Bad* (Figure 3.23).

P1:   (*written*) Hi. You give a lot of examples of people and groups that you would think would be more likely than others to think critically across the board, yet the evidence seems to show that they don't. Does education level make any real difference, then?

AU: (*written*) Yes, I do believe education can make a difference, but our evolutionary heritage will make us all inconsistent...

P1:   (*written*) **Have you noticed** that students have gotten better or worse at CT?

AU: (*written*) I am currently teaching a CT class, and I see students making progress as the semester unfolds. Yet, when the context is changed (for example, from paranormal claims to a psychological claim), they struggle applying CT in the new context.

Mod: (*written*) Question was: You give a lot of examples of people and groups that you would think would be more likely than others to think critically across the board, yet the evidence seems to show that they don't. Does education level make any real difference, then?

Figure 3.23   Task design in corralling

P2:   (*written*) That's pretty similar to the question that I was going to ask, which is, Is critical thinking something that can be taught? Don't you need to have a certain temperament or outlook and, if so, what kind of temperament do students need?

P3:   (*written*) You also spoke briefly of the role gender and race may play in CT, **could you expand on that?**

AU: (*written*) Students need to be teachable. Sort of like an athlete needs to be coachable. If they are willing to learn, then I believe anyone can become a CT... Not sure where I addressed the role of gender and race in CT...

Mod: (*written*) Author said earlier that he is not a lightning-fast typist so bare with him. ☺ Now me, on the other hand, I type lightning-fast, but say the wrong things as a result.

P1:   (*written*) I was going to ask why students are adept with the paranormal criticism but not with psychological stuff.

Mod: (*written*) **Perhaps** CT needs to be taught at a MUCH earlier age than it currently is. By high school or college we've already developed bad thinking habits.

P3:   (*written*) You talked about the disproportionate number of males in groups such as the Skeptics Society.

AU: (*written*) The way I teach the course, we cover paranormal claims first (it's exciting to students)... Yet, they all seem to struggle when a new topic area occurs. I have not met many skeptics that apply CT to economic claims, so perhaps it is not just students who have this issue.

P1:   (*written*) **That's a good point**, Moderator. **Yet** teachers are often criticized for teaching that way – not the 'content'.

P4:   (*written*) Yes, teachers are not critical thinkers themselves in the primary education level. They tend to discourage CT in their students.

AU: (*written*) Yes, I think CT should be taught very early (Santa is a great way to do it!). I used the disproportionate number of males in Skeptical organizations as an example of applying one set of standards in one situation, while not applying them to ourselves...

This excerpt illustrates how chat can be an excellent tool for teaching students the language appropriate for a formal discussion. By example, the teacher/moderator can corral learners into applying language such as 'Have you noticed...', 'Could you expand on that...', 'Perhaps...', 'That's a good point, yet...' and the like, all necessary for conducting a coherent discussion while expressing respect for others' opinions and thoughts.

Example: Live author chat on CNN (social studies)

Such live author chats can be used as opportunities for students to design thoughtful questions and for teachers to corral them into developing and posing them. http://www.cnn.com/COMMUNITY/transcripts/2001/04/04/michelherbeck/

In this example, questions were asked by a chat participant in a moderated chat conversation with authors Lou Michel and Dan Herbeck, authors of a book about Timothy McVeigh: Do you feel that your book gives unwarranted attention to McVeigh? Have you heard from any of the victims' families, either for or against this book being published? Does McVeigh have a following of anti-government people? Any supporters? Do you think McVeigh acted alone? This illustrates how students can be asked to come up with interesting questions and ask them during such an activity.

Example: Supervolcano: What's under Yellowstone? (middle and high school geography)

http://www.discovery.com/

Chat activities can be arranged not only with book authors but also experts from different fields or simply people of interest from all walks of life from around the world. The following excerpt from a live chat with two volcanologists illustrates this. The chat activity was preceded by students watching a Discovery video and was followed by their converting the results of the chat into a short paper. For such a paper, students can be corralled into using the target scientific concepts and terminology learned via chatting.

P: (*written*) I've read that many **trails** in Yellowstone are over 200 degrees and **magma** is only three-tenths of a mile below the **surface**. Doesn't that seem a little ominous?

V: (*written*) First of all, I would question how many **trails** in Yellowstone are at boiling temperature, and then I would also question that **depth of magma**. The best **seismic imaging** shows the closest **magma** in Yellowstone to be on the order of three to four miles below the **surface**. The only **trails** that we know are hot are those in **geyser**

basins where the **geyser basin** itself is very hot. Many times, the Park Service places boardwalks over the hot ground so that visitors can still enjoy the very beautiful **thermal features**.

Example: Velocity (high school physics)

https://www.physicsforums.com/

The written nature of chats allows for quick reference and the corralling of students into using outside sources. Students can also be corralled into interpreting their results and adopting the vocabulary used in them. The following chat from a physics class is an example of this (Figure 3.24).

S1: (*written*) Does 1 car hitting a wall at 120mph=2 cars colliding, each going 60mph?

S2: (*written*) No. The **kinetic energy** of an object is equal to 1/2mv^2. Thus, the situation with the car going 120mph actually has twice the **kinetic energy** of the two cars each going 60mph.

S3: (*written*) Question answered with 5:47 video that makes it very clear and intuitive why the answer is no. http://www.youtube.com/watch?v=r8E5d...eature=related.

Example: Math chat

http://www.artofproblemsolving.com/School/mathjams.php?mj_id=260

T: (*written*) Let's try another problem.

$$\text{Compute: } \frac{5!6!}{6!+5!+5!}$$

The exclamation point is a 'factorial'. 4!=4×3×2×1, and factorials for all other positive integers are defined similarly – we multiply all the numbers from the given positive integer down to 1. **Do we have to multiply all that out to evaluate the given expression?**

S1: (*written*) No!

S2: (*written*) factor out the 5!

S3: (*written*) no! factor 5! from the top and bottom

S4: (*written*) no, we can use factorization

S5: (*written*) no, we can factor out 5! on the bottom

S6: (*written*) factor out 5! from all terms on the denominator

T: (*written*) **We don't have to multiply. We can factor instead. How can we factor the denominator?**

S4: (*written*) each of the terms have 5!, thus we have 5!(6+1+1)

S8: (*written*) 5!(6+1+1)

S7: (*written*) 5!(6+1+1)

S5: (*written*) 5!(6+1+1)=5!(8)

S9: (*written*) 5!(6+1+1)=5!(8)

T: (*written*) **Excellent; that's how we factor the denominator. So, how do we finish the problem?**

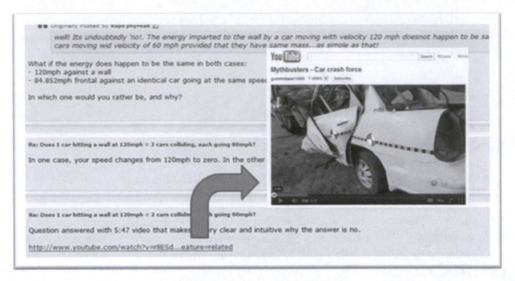

Figure 3.24   Structuring task in chat

S1:   (*written*) then we can cross out the 5! from the numerator and the denominator

S6:   (*written*) since 5! is = 5*4*3*2*1 we could simplify this by dividing the top and the bottom with 5!

T: (*written*) **And what do we get?**

S7:   (*written*) 720/8=90

S4:   (*written*) so its 6!/8 which is 90

S2:   (*written*) cancel the 5! and there's a 6!/8

T: (*written*)

> the denominator can factor like so:
>
> $$6! + 5! + 5! = 6 \times 5! + 5! + 5! = (6 + 1 + 1)5! = 8 \times 5!$$
>
> Now our problem is much easier:
>
> $$\frac{5!6!}{6! + 5! + 5!} = \frac{5!6!}{8 \times 5!} = \frac{6!}{8} = 90.$$
>
> Know your factorials from 1! up to 8!)

Also, clever factoring is extremely useful in math problems, and is often helpful in MATHCOUNTS.

This teacher does not provide students with all the right answers but rather teaches by engaging and supporting guided practice, step-by-step interactional problem-solving and checking for understanding and redirecting as needed.

Corralling projects in chats

Text-based chats can be a great place for students working on small-group projects to get together in real time and work collaboratively on details. This type of activity is more suitable for high school students.

Example: Solar power and hydropower (high school geography)

S1:   (*written*) So what sources will we choose?

S2:   (*written*) I like the hydropower topic. There are looots of pics on the Net we can use.

S1:   (*written*) I like this, too. What examples do you know? I'm googling right now. Here is the article about the hydropower plants with images.

S2:   (*written*) Just don't use Wikipedia.

S1:   (*written*) Why not? They have some nice links. Just look http://en.wikipedia.org/wiki/Hydropower.

S1:   (*written*) Links are fine but not the content. Actually I just opened it and there is a nice image of the inside we can look at.

This example, as well as those that preceded it, demonstrate that the affordances of each medium can be utilized to reach the instructional goal.

Corralling in text chats: section summary

The real-time nature of text chats makes opportunities for active corralling elusive but, as we have seen, not impossible. Both students and instructors detected teachable moments and used the text chat format to steer learners into productive thinking and expression.

Conclusion

It is clear from the preceding examples that the four online venues – VoiceThread, audio/video conferences, discussion forums and text chats – as well as various combinations of these can be employed creatively and constructively. They are ideal spaces to exercise the instructional conversation strategy of corralling student learning. Each of these environments has indisputably powerful affordances that, with thoughtful instruction, can have a significant impact on the way students learn when they are appropriately corralled into conducting specific tasks using discipline-focused discourse. Designing and carrying out instruction and instructional conversations promote involved participation and, consequently, academic development. As we have illustrated, the critical players in corralling learning activities remain the excellent educators who plan, orchestrate and guide learners while using corralling in their online instructional conversations.

End-of-chapter activities

(1) Ask a friend, family member or classmate to do some live role play with you. The goal will be to practice instructional corralling. Choose one or all of the following to use as the focal learning. Then, engage your volunteer in instructional conversation on the topic while steering them into making active use of the target idea and term.

- Brining and pickling are examples of food preservation.

- From our perspective on Earth, what happens when the Moon's shadow crosses the Earth's surface (solar eclipse), or when the Moon moves into the Earth's shadow (lunar eclipse).

   Debrief with your partner, probing if and how your strategies could be improved.

(2) Do the same as (1) but online using a live chat venue and an asynchronous text or voice venue.

(3) View a handful of YouTube how-to videos. Can you find instances whereby the person doing the instructing corrals either you the viewer or someone on camera into learning?

(4) With a partner, choose one of this chapter's illustrations of corralling and discuss how you might modify it (change the content, the grade level) for use in your own teaching.

Further reading

Cope, B. and Kalantzis, M. (2013) 'Multiliteracies': New literacies new learning. In M. Hawkins (ed.) *Framing Languages and Literacies: Socially Situated Views and Perspectives* (pp. 105–135). New York: Routledge.

Gynne, A. and Bagga-Gupta, S. (2015) Languaging in the twenty-first century: Exploring varieties and modalities in literacies inside and outside learning spaces. *Language and Education* 29 (6), 509–526.

Kalantzis, M. and Cope, B. (2010) The teacher as designer: Pedagogy in the new media age. *E-learning and Digital Media* 7 (3), 200–222.

Kitson, L., Fletcher, M. and Kearney, J. (2007) Continuity and change in literacy practices: A move towards multiliteracies. *The Journal of Classroom Interaction* 41 (2), 29–41.

Meskill, C. and Anthony, N. (2004–2005) Teaching and learning with telecommunications: Forms of instructional discourse in a hybrid Russian class. *Journal of Educational Technology Systems* 33 (2), 103–109.

Meskill, C. and Anthony, N. (2007) The language of teaching well with learning objects. *Journal of Online Learning and Teaching* 3 (1), 79–93.

Messina Dahlberg, G. and Bagga-Gupta, S. (2014) Understanding glocal learning spaces. An empirical study of languaging and transmigrant positions in the virtual classroom. *Learning, Media and Technology* 39 (4), 468–487.

References

Brunvand, S. and Byrd, S. (2011) Using VoiceThread to promote learning engagement and success for all students. *Teaching Exceptional Children* 43 (4), 28–37.

Kim, H. and Bonk, C. (2010) Toward best practices in online teaching: Instructional immediacy in online faculty experiences. *International Journal of Instructional Technology and Distance Learning* 7 (8), 31–44.

Meskill, C. and Anthony, N. (2005) Foreign language learning with CMC: Forms of online instructional discourse in a hybrid Russian Class. *System* 33 (1), 89–105.

Meskill, C. and Anthony, N. (2015) *Teaching Languages Onlin (2nd edn)*. Bristol: Multilingual Matters.

Wood, K.D., Stover, K. and Kissel, B. (2013) Using digital VoiceThreads to promote 21st century learning. *Middle School Journal* 44 (4), 58–64.

4

Orchestrating interactions and scaffolding synthetic thinking

In this chapter you will learn:

- the anatomy of encouraging interactions and synthetic thinking as an instructional conversation strategy;

- the special affordances of synchronous forums (voicethreads, discussion forums, audio/video conferences and text-based chats) for encouraging interactions and synthetic thinking;

- how encouraging interactions and synthetic thinking as an instructional conversation strategy can be undertaken in a range of online environments;

- how these environments' affordances can be taken advantage of to support and amplify these conversations.

About orchestrating interactions and scaffolding synthetic thinking

In the brief yet frenetic history of online teaching and learning, one aspect of pedagogy continues to rise to the fore. Both instructors and learners consistently point to the pleasure, richness and effectiveness of online interactions: instructor–student and student–students (Picciano, 2002). Fully online and blended courses that capitalize on these dynamics, both synchronously and asynchronously, are highly satisfying for all involved. Students consistently rate these elements of their online experiences as the most important to their learning. Moreover, well-orchestrated interaction between and among learners and instructors can lead to deeper understanding of the target content and to the subject matter fluency that accompanies this understanding. By productively using content language and concepts, learners come to own these as their own (Freeman *et al.*, 2014). Further, instructors and students can scaffold one another toward *synthetic thinking* and expression (Saunders *et al.*, 1992). In the following sections, we illustrate and discuss the online instructional conversation strategies of orchestrating interactions and scaffolding synthetic thinking.

Orchestrating interactions and scaffolding synthetic thinking with voice

The asynchronous nature of VoiceThread lends itself well to encouraging learners to interact with one another for active problem-solving with synthetic thinking the result. Synthetic thinking can develop out of actively orchestrated interactions such as debating different aspects of a problem to be solved. By designing and orchestrating tasks that require learners to think and explore the main topic from a range of perspectives, students become involved in investigating multiple facets of the same phenomenon. Learners and their instructor can jointly construct the eventual synthesis of this information to develop the larger conceptual picture. In doing so, students actively learn to understand and apply the gradually complexifying disciplinary discourse that is attendant to the content area.

Orchestrating interactions using target definitions

Interactions among students within asynchronous voice applications are a great way to concentrate on subject-specific definitions and to push learners to productively incorporate these in their online work. The time affordances of the medium again allow for the careful crafting of oral messages and responses to others' questions.

Example: Naproxen (middle school)

In this VoiceThread activity, Naproxen, a pair of students was given an assignment to make a presentation on one of a list of existing drugs and answer questions about that drug from the rest of the group. In doing so, those students who played the role of experts and those who played the role of novices actively employed a number of disciplinary-specific terms such as *hormones, side effects, cholesterol, steroidal, inflammation,* etc. This not only broadened their knowledge of the particular drug and synthesized its different working mechanisms, but also allowed them to exercise expert language while doing so (Figure 4.1).

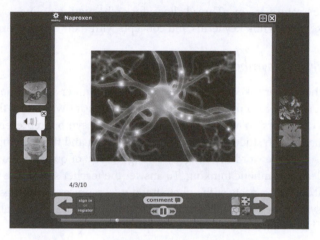

Figure 4.1 Orchestrating interactions using target definitions in VoiceThread

S1: (*oral*) Naproxis are included in the group of drugs known as **non-steroidal anti-flammatory** drugs or insets. They work by reducing **hormones** in the body that cause inflammation and pain.

S2: (*oral*) I was wondering if naproxen like other inset was reacted with **cholesterol lowering** drugs to produce other negative **side effects**.

S1: (*oral*) To answer your question, there are not been any known interactions between naproxen and **cholesterol lowering** drugs known as statins.

S3: (*oral*) When you said that the hormone level would be lowered when using this drug, I was wondering how it would affect teenagers whose **hormones** are all over the place.

S1: (*oral*) To answer your question, the **hormones** we were talking about were prostaglandins that are tissues that control blood pressure, muscle contraction, and also the modulation of **inflammation**.

S4: (*oral*) What happens if you take naproxen and you don't have any swallowing going on? Would it have any **aversive effects**?

S1: (*oral*) Since the naproxen is used as a swallowing reducer and as a pain reliever, if you don't have any swallowing and just pain, you can still use it if you don't have any **side effects**.

By asking questions that prompted students to elaborate further on the ideas they expressed, the instructor took advantage of the medium to focus and extend learners' thinking and collaborations. While this is a common instructional conversation strategy in traditional classrooms, the asynchronous nature of VoiceThread provided the teacher opportunities to more readily notice teachable moments and afforded her the time to craft instructionally powerful responses. She thus orchestrated the kinds of conversation that both promoted and revealed learning.

Orchestrating synthetic thinking using a key term

The asynchronous nature of VoiceThread allows for orchestrating online conversations so that students take time to link key terms and concepts with their own life experiences.

Example: Analysis of symbolism (high school)

In this activity, the teacher asked her student to comment on her slides. She asked the following questions: Where and when does the symbol appear? What does the symbol mean to various characters? What larger meaning does this symbol represent throughout the play? Noticing that the student mentioned a photograph and the warning it represents, the teacher focused on the word 'warning' by asking a series of questions to orchestrate the conversation to lead to synthetic thinking. To answer the teacher's post, the student had to think about what specific aspects of the photograph may represent warnings. The student was thus led to synthesize her own life experiences with what she learned about this play and its author (Figure 4.2).

Figure 4.2   Encouraging synthetic thinking using a key term in VoiceThread

S: (*oral*) The photograph of Amanda's husband hangs over peninsula in the house. So it served as a reminder to what might happen to the family if Laura doesn't find the gentleman caller to provide for her mother. It also represents what Tom might become if he does not conform his mother's wishes. And the picture loomed over every scene in the play and serving as a warning and a reminder.

T: (*oral*) I liked how you pointed out that the photograph is also a **warning**, and I was wondering what it might be **warning**. Is it **warning** us that Tom might leave and be like the father or is it the **warning** to Tom?

The teacher engages this student in further interactions by making connections between a key word in the student's post, the student's comprehension of the book, and the student's own life experience.

Orchestrating interactions and synthetic thinking

VoiceThread activities can be nicely tailored to learners' ages and stages of development. Even young children can develop skills in synthesizing pieces of knowledge and applying concepts they have learned previously to new situations.

Example: Fourth-grade art

The art teacher launched this VoiceThread with the purpose of engaging her fourth graders in conversation about their individual art projects and those of well-known professional artists. Students commented on their own and others' presentations about art. At one point, a student applied the concept of symbolism, something he had obviously learned in this art class. Another student readily took up the lead and developed the idea of symbolism, using her own example (Figure 4.3).

Figure 4.3   Encouraging interactions and synthetic thinking in VoiceThread

S1: *(oral)* In the Ramayana, the king dies and the Ram's father remarries. Rum's step-mother banishes him to the forest for fourteen year. Burrato, Rum's stepbrother, does not want to be the new king. So he asks Rum to give him his **slipper** so the people would who the real king is.

S2: *(oral)* The **shoe** is a **symbol** to represent Rum's true world over the land of Ayodiah. Can you think of other stories that use **shoes as symbols**?

S3: *(oral)* Yes! The ruby slippers are **symbolic objects** in the Wizard of Oz. I always thought it's a way to get this. Some believe it **represents** the inner sparking of all of us. It could also be a **symbol** of the power of belief.

S4: *(orally)* Another story that uses **shoes as a symbol** is Cinderella. The glass slippers **represent** Cinderella's delicate nature. The person who can wear these shoes must be physically fit.

In tandem with the teacher's orchestration, the asynchronous nature of this medium of communication allowed students to take the time they needed to make connections with previous statements, analyze their classmates' postings and compose their own responses while making productive use of discipline-specific vocabulary.

Orchestrating interactions outside the classroom

VoiceThread is an excellent venue for students to interact in using subject-specific discourse beyond the classroom. Interacting with others is, after all, an authentic way to extend one's verbal and written mastery of targeted language and concepts.

Example: After Chernobyl (middle and high school)

As in this example, teachers can refer their students to VoiceThread based on global concepts that build on and extend the school curriculum. These kinds of 'beyond the classroom' online conversations are reflected in this example about Chernobyl (Figure 4.4).

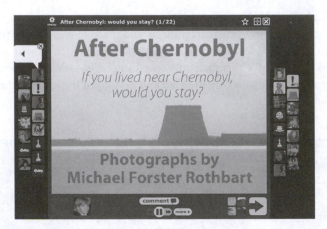

Figure 4.4   Encouraging interactions outside classroom in VoiceThread

AU: (*oral*) I am Michael Forster and I'm a photojournalist. For the past two years I've being photographing people who live near the Chernobyl accident site. I want to understand why so many people are still living and working around Chernobyl now, a generation after the accident. The first thing you have to know about this web site is that it's designed to be interactive. I don't want you just to sit and watch. I want to start a conversation here. So please share reactions to these photos or share your own memories about Chernobyl.

P1:   (*oral*) I think most people have stayed because where else they are going to go. They wouldn't be able to sell their property to anybody else and get any kind of money for it, probably. They'd lose all the savings. In addition, they've already been exposed to the radiation. So staying probably is not going to add any to the exposure they've already had.

P2:   (*oral*) Of course, I would not stay. I'd have to look after my family. Obviously, this is not a rational question.

P3:   (*oral*) Chernobyl happened so on and go that even the radiation is still leaked out and they tried to clean it up, it's still high. So staying would probably be a bad choice. So I probably would have left but people may stayed because it's their home town.

Conversing with people with a range of perspectives on such a life-changing event is clearly an enthralling activity. Considering and analyzing polar points of view can be critically important for students in developing skills in listening and responding intelligently.

Orchestrating interactions by requiring student questions

Explicitly requiring students to generate thoughtful questions to pose to one another works well in VoiceThread for the many reasons we've already cited regarding time for preparation and review. Further, student-posed questions help grease the conversational wheels and sustain learner interest and participation as we can see in the following example.

Example: Lily's crossing (elementary school)

Here, the teacher instructed her students to respond to their classmates' postings and also to ask a question they would like their classmates to respond to. This initiated a *multiparty conversation* whereby students eagerly asked and answered the questions posted not only by their teacher but also by their classmates.

T: (*oral*) Lily and Margaret are best friends but the two of them together means trouble.

S1:   (*oral*) I agree. Lily and Margaret together do mean trouble. First of all, they try to sneak into the movie theater to see the show three times even though it was successful all three times. **Would you try to sneak into the movie theater?**

S2:   (*oral*) Margaret saw the bag of candy they were going to send him next. So she shared some with Lily. **Do you think guys it was a good idea?**

S3:   (*oral*) For one thing, I agree with you, Mrs Teacher. These two together are trouble. But to answer your question, Student 1, I don't think it was a very good idea that they kept sneaking into the movie theater. It would have been kind of fun at first to watch the movie three times and not get caught but after a while it could get boring. Alex got caught. That's not risk I would take. But **to answer your** question, Student 2, **I don't think it's a very good idea** that they eat candy but they kind of needed them in Europe because they don't have that kind of stuff over there.

S4:   (*oral*) Lily and Margaret are both trouble. If I were in that candy situation, I would get in big trouble. **If you were in that situation, what do you think would happen?**

S1:   (*oral*) To answer your question, Student 4, **if I were in that candy situation,** I would be in huge trouble. I was sharing with my friend just like Margaret's Mom did, my Mom would tell me that my friend was trouble and I should stay away from them and I would get bunch of my privileges taken away and I would be grounded for the rest of my life most likely.

S2:   (*oral*) **If I was caught in that situation** oh boy my parents would ground me for a really long time. They probably not let me see or play with my friends anymore. And they would be really disappointed in me I bet because I think they believe in me and they trust me a lot more.

Students readily answered one another's questions with great interest and asked their own questions. They had the time to compose and carefully edit them in this asynchronous medium.

Orchestrating interactions with incidental student questions

Questions can also be raised on tangential topics during oral asynchronous discussions. As in the next example, students might digress from the focal topic in order to discuss a particular aspect of the subject that interests them, something that can be awkward to do in live classrooms due to time constraints. This venue, however, allows for such incidental instructional opportunities between peers.

Example: The Journal of Scott Pendleton Collins

While discussing *The Journal of Scott Pendleton Collins*, students were focused on answering the question of whether it is justifiable to go to war just because your ancestors had. During the discussion, one of the students digressed from the topic by asking questions about the censorship of letters. This obviously interested others. The discussion did not veer from developing students' analytical abilities. On the contrary, talking about a tangential issue appeared to motivate interest even further on the focal content.

S1: (*oral*) Scott went to war because his ancestors did. Would you do the same? Why or why not?

S2: (*oral*) I would do it because I'm fighting for my country and if you fight for your country, you'd kind of be rewarded for fighting for your country because you get your picture upon the wall.

S3: (*oral*) Yes, I would because I would want to carry on my family's culture and make it into a tradition.

S4: (*oral*) I agree with Student 1 but I also think you shouldn't do just because your ancestors did. You should do it because you want to.

S1: (*oral*) I would do the same because when I am older my children would look up to me with pride.

S3: (*oral*) **Do you think they are censoring the letters?**

S5: (*oral*) I would not like to go to war because I would not like to get killed like my ancestors did. **I think they are censoring** the letters because if the Germans got it, they would know where the Americans were.

S2: (*oral*) **I think they are not censoring** the letters because they are busy doing other stuff and don't have time to send letters and yet I think they are censoring the letters because there might be something that is not appropriate and if there is something inappropriate in the letter, they probably would not send it anyway.

The students not only asked and responded to questions about censorship, but also supplied their reasoning, an academic discourse pattern that is becoming more and more central in academic assessments.

Orchestrating synthetic thinking via student projects

Synthetic thinking is something that can be orchestrated via conversations about student-made online multimedia projects.

Example: Objects in the sky (third grade)

In this whole-class project about celestial objects, each of the students adds a piece of information to the knowledge-building activity, thus generating the larger picture collaboratively. They are focused on listening to each other's postings in order to produce their own observations and avoid repetition (Figure 4.5).

Figure 4.5 Encouraging synthetic thinking in student project with VoiceThread

S1: (*oral*) When you look at the Moon with the telescope, you can see many craters.
S2: (*oral*) The Moon doesn't make its own light.
S3: (*oral*) When the Moon is gone, that means it is a new moon.
S4: (*oral*) Did you know it takes up to 28 days to a month for the Moon to go around the Earth.
S5: (*oral*) The craters on the Moon are from long ago meteoroids that hit the Moon.

During these kinds of interactions, students reinforce their knowledge by employing subject-specific vocabulary and teaching one another new facts about the Moon.

Orchestrating interactions and scaffolding synthetic thinking with voice: section summary

In the preceding examples, we saw how the asynchronous nature of voiceboards and voicethreads can be used to encourage learners to interact with new content and with one another, interactions that lead to practice with, development of and clear evidence of synthetic thinking. Instructors can make use of such evidence in holistic assessments of individual student progress in a thematic unit and/or for summative assessments and further curricular and instructional planning.

Orchestrating interactions and scaffolding synthetic thinking with text

Instructional communication in text-based asynchronous environments can be designed and shaped to focus on learners interacting with one another and the target content. The medium permits the teacher to make time-independent decisions regarding just how she wishes to orchestrate the learner interactions using carefully crafted written messages. Likewise, she can store and track evidence of individual and group learning and its development into synthetic thinking.

Orchestrating interactions and synthetic thinking by directing

When students are asked to produce and post their reflections on a subject, they tend to express their own opinions without referring to their classmates' postings. In order to ensure that successful interactions are maintained throughout a discussion topic, the instructor can use a number of techniques that capitalize on the asynchronous textual mode of instruction. One strategy is to simply direct students to respond to one another. Building in evaluations and grade weights for student–student responses also motivates learners and can get them into the habit of attending to one another's posts conversationally.

Example: Writing class (middle school)

The teacher in this example started the topic *Earth as a Utopia* in her writing class. To prompt her students to read each other's messages, she specifically instructed them to respond to someone else's posting and to interact with this person.

T: (*written*) We can all think of things that would make the world a better place, like eliminating disease and starvation. What are some of your ideas about what would make the world a better place? What things would you want to get rid of? What would you like to change about the culture we live in? Your job this week is to write a paragraph of no less than six sentences about what you think would make our world a utopia? **You should then respond to another peer's ideas and dialogue with them.**

S1:   (*written*) Even though our world is trying to be 'A more perfect union' we still have many flaws. I would change our world **hunger problem**; I would also solve the **Racist problem** in America so we can all be truly 'created equal'. I would destroy all **drugs** excluding medical drugs, drugs such as Cocaine, Marijuana, exc. Then I would proceed to **change the law system**, like changing the penalty's of crimes. Our culture wouldn't need much changing in matters of keeping each countries culture. I would also **abolish war**, in every part of the world by taking out the army and focusing more on helping the environment and less about killing each other.

S2:   (*written*) Student 1, I agree with most of your points including the **racism** and **drugs**. Those I feel are 'hot topics' in our modern society that nobody is coming out and trying to deal with, like in northern Florida there is a high school that still has **segregated proms**.

S3:   (*written*) I think that we should **eliminate waste** in our world. Maybe make a way to where all food and packaging it edible. The reason I think that is because a lot of people trash the earth with their trash and it's not right. Also somehow it gets in the ocean and kills the animals. If there was a way to make this all come true I would totally make it happen. Waste is a big problem in our world today so that is what I would change in my utopia.

S4:   (*written*) Student 3, I agree with **eliminating waste** and how people don't throw their trash away. Waste does kill many animals each year and pollutes our air.

Students followed their teacher's directive and picked up using the targeted concepts from their classmates' postings. In reading and thinking about one another's ideas, they evaluate other points of view critically, constructively and synthetically.

Orchestrating anchored interactions

Asynchronous text-based discussion forums are excellent venues for encouraging anchored interactions among students. Such anchors include embedded images, videos or charts and links to various online sources. Recall also that task toolkits serve as excellent anchors.

Example: Is intelligence inherited (high school biology)

In this example, a biology teacher reflected on her student's post about the origins of intelligence and in turn orchestrated a discussion among her students. Students eagerly responded to both the students' and the teacher's posts arguing against the notion that intelligence is inherited. They supported their positions by providing links to a Yahoo group that was discussing the same topic and to a site with quotes.

S1:   (*written*) (*posted her critique about intelligence being inherited*)

T: (*written*) I really like that you brought this discussion to the blog, Student 1. Many students already buy into this concept that intelligence is predetermined (and like to use it as an excuse for not doing well – 'I'm just no good at INSERT SUBJECT HERE'). I'm not convinced at all. In fact, in a future post I'll provide a counterpoint to Dr Bouchard's claims. Also, just want to point out that IQ (what was measured in the study) does not necessarily correspond with success in school or in adult life. **But, if intelligence is largely inherited, wouldn't it be a polygenic trait rather than controlled by a single gene due to the multiple ranges in intelligence seen?**

S2:   (*written*) Wow, good post. I agree with Teacher, about the polygenic trait part. I mean how one gene could hold all the intelligence that has been passed down from your parents. Also wouldn't the parents of a special ed kid be 'dumb'. Well I was a little confused so went and did some research and this is the website i thought provided great examples and evidence. http://sg.answers.yahoo.com/question/index?qid=2007 0117072939AAqeKxj&show=7.

S3:   (*written*) It is true that work ethic has everything to do with it. Albert Einstein said, 'It's not that I'm so smart, it's just that I stay with problems longer'. This just shows that those who are lazy and give up do not have the drive to succeed. http://www.brainyquote.com/quotes/quotes/a/alberteins106192.html.

Accustomed to the malleable and accessible nature of online venues of communication, these students took full advantage of the anchoring possibilities to support their ideas and positions.

Orchestrating interactions and synthetic thinking with provocative topics

To teach students how to delineate and evaluate arguments and specific claims in a text, teachers can asynchronously guide students to read and evaluate each other's postings to identify and comment on claims made. Orchestrating these kinds of interactions can mean using provocative topics to encourage lively meaningful discussion.

Example: European history (high school)

The teacher started a discussion on the topic *Do You Wanna Start a Revolution!?*, asking students to provide arguments and supporting evidence in their messages. As the topic called for students' personal opinions, it stimulated just such a productive discussion where arguments and warrants naturally occur.

S1:   (*written*) even though the world had seen **democracies** before, the American **Revolution** showed the Europeans what it's like to really have one. The American **Revolution** also brought tyranny within the kingdom, and caused more **philosophers' ideas** to be recognized.
S2:   (*written*) **Revolution** doesn't **solve** anything.
S3:   (*written*) **Revolutions solved** things for them....
S4:   (*written*) If there was not a **revolution** there would be no United States.
S5:   (*written*) How did it cause more **philosophers ideas** to be recognized?...
S6:   (*written*) Yay, someone else knew about previous **democracies**!
S7:   (*written*) in some cases a **Revolution** does **solve** things but in other cases they don't, it depends on why they started the **revolution**.
S6:   (*written*) **Revolutions** do **solve** problems by creating more problems that people will find out years later are serious problems. They are a **temporary solution** to a serious problem. They also give you the chance to fix the **problem** for good though. Eventually they do **solve** problems.

Orchestrating mutual feedback with target terms

One of the best ways to involve students in instructional interactions is to assign them to comment on each other's work. The textual nature of the medium allows students to attend to each other's postings while taking as much time and care as they need. They can also take as much time as they need to compose appropriate answers.

Example: Chemistry 1: Comment on your classmates' websites

This chemistry teacher assigned students to provide feedback to at least one chemistry website created by their classmates. Students followed the teacher's lead and included numerous web-design specific vocabulary items and thus practiced them in a meaningful way.

T: (*written*) Is there anything that you do not fully understand about the atom? Curious what another group's take on your topic was? Read what your classmates learned and comment on it here. Feel free to give warm or cool feedback, just be polite. Although projects are organized by class, feel free to read and comment on projects from other class sections. **My goal is for everyone to read and comment on at least one other topic/website.**

S1: (*written*) Since we did our website on the big bang theory, i decided to check out the big bang project from section yellow. I think that Ada & Katherine did very well on their website. The website had a ton of **information** that was on topic and on an academic level we could all understand. Also they had many **pictures and diagrams**, which made it very pleasant to look at and to learn from. The only suggestion i would make is to have links at the end of each **sub-page** to take you back to the first one, just to make **viewing the website** easier.

S2: (*written*) Since my partner and I had Dalton's Atomic Theory, I decided to take a look at that webpage by the other two sections. I think that their website is pretty well-done. I really like how Emily and Angelica compared Dalton to other scientists and talked about what he originally studied. One suggestion I have would be to use more **'reader-friendly' colors**, maybe something darker and easier to read as opposed to the neon turquoise on the website.

Students attended to both the content and the form of their classmates' productions, both essential skills for critique. In this case, students pointed to the strengths and weaknesses of their projects and employed reasoning.

Example: America underneath (middle school social studies)

Students listened to a presentation on different segments of American culture presented by one of the students in the form of a voice presentation. The student pointed out both positive and negative cultural aspects. The class then discussed both the pluses and minuses of her presentation. The teacher corralled students into using reasoning and providing additional evidence for the arguments in their posts.

S1: (*oral*) (*made a presentation about different parts of American culture*)

S2: (*written*) While I agree with your commentary on the economic situation of many Americans, I disagree with your view that Americans are there to help each other. The Americans in bad economics situations neither get help from the government, nor their countrymen.

S3: (*written*) I agree mostly with your presentation. I disagree that some people's misfortune isn't their fault. If they had tried earlier in life to become successful, they wouldn't be in the situation they are in now.

S4:   (*written*) I agree with both the good and bad parts of your point but I can connect the most with the bad parts. There is hidden poverty and pollution that is 'fixed' quickly. The bad parts of America are hidden in some ways but at the same time they are obvious in everything we do. The diners are good in that they create economic opportunities but at the same time the people who work there are stuck their without much opportunity to get out and also it does indeed show the laziness of many Americans. The bad America is hidden behind the good.

This activity clearly engaged students in writing arguments to support claims with clear reasons and relevant evidence.

Structuring interactions with initial questions

Structuring student interactions with a set of questions they are supposed to respond to collectively works particularly well with asynchronous text. It is one way of engaging students in a conversation that, while structured, gives plenty of room for free expression.

Example: Censorship debate (middle school)

To encourage the development of reasoning skills and increase students' ability to actually comprehend and argue with their classmates' opinions in academically acceptable ways, introducing discussion forums with tasks containing several 'why' questions is an effective strategy.

T: (*written*) Read and listen to any threads already posted and then write at least two threads responding to the following questions: (1) **Why** and how should language be censored? (2) **Why** should language never be censored? Your responses should introduce **new**, **legitimate** ideas to the debate.

S1:   (*written*) **I agree** with my classmate on the fact that censorship can be and is well used for example in the kids' shows. **But I also think** that words like the 'F' word is often censored and we all know what they are saying and we all know this word since a very long time. Some shows, as the dating shows on MTV are cut every 2 seconds but it does not stop people from watching them. **Also**, censorship can be dangerous, the 'bad' word eliminated are generally accepted as a protection for children, but on a larger scale, someone who controls can ban some words for example in a speech or in song.

S2:   (*written*) **Like previously stated posts**, language should be censored in order to omit inappropriate language from society. Language, in a sense, is already censored in the media when shows are pre-recorded and words can be chosen, or censored. Subconsciously, we also censor language when we choose to think before we speak, or when we consider how our diction will affect those around us. When it comes to the media, language can be censored when the editors or directors of a particular show choose to omit certain phrases for whatever reason, especially when it comes to offensive issues. **I also think** language should be censored when it seems irrelevant. The news often includes redundant stories, when there are more important matters to worry about. **But again**, this is bias on the editor's part, so language cannot be accurate AND censored.

S3: (*written*) **I agree** with most others, who say that shows/movies and book which are aimed at kids should be censored. Small kids do not understand all of the 'adult' content which is sometimes illustrated in television shows, movies, and songs. **But** too much censorship isn't good either. A child whose parents are too 'overprotective' may become curious in the movies/music/games that his or her friend is allowed to watch. **Then**, if seeing these materials without the parent's permission, the kid would have a huge wake up call. Kids need to be introduced to new concepts slowly. Even if the media is censored for the protection of children, there are always other ways children can obtain new information, such as from the older kids on a school bus. Another example is when an adult, who isn't usually around children swears while talking around one. **My point to this** is that yes, Television, video games and music should be censored because of young kids, but it would be very difficult to censor all language. It's impossible for inappropriate material to be removed from a child's life completely, but censoring certain parts, may help the child be introduced to more mature contents slowly.

By structuring student-to-student interactions with a set of questions, students are corralled into using lexical and syntactic constructions appropriate for expressing the reasons and steps in their thought processes.

Structuring interactions with redirecting questions

Teachers can orchestrate discussions by redirecting questions, making thought-provoking statements and providing imaginative examples. They can simultaneously structure student interactions to make them focused and appropriate. Redirecting questions is one strategy to accomplish this.

Example: Absolutism (high school in Japan)

T: (*written*) **Do you believe that an Absolute Monarch could be good for a society?** Explain your answer and respond to another class member's answer

S1: (*written*) An absolute monarch could be good for a society because it can control the society better however, having an unlimited amount of power could be a disadvantage because it can create conflict or rebellion to other people about the control they are having in the country. And possible reasons for conflict maybe because of the ideas between the countries and that particular leader could be different or certain laws or decisions that are decided by the leader could affect peoples' lives. If the absolute monarch had all the characteristics of a good leader, I would reckon it would stabilize the society and having people to look up at you more as a leader.

T: (*written*) So Student 1 **what you are saying is that is an Absolute Monarch had the ability and the desire to help a society that an Absolute Monarch would be good for the country. If the Absolute Monarch is selfish or a bad leader than it would be bad for the country. Is that correct?** If so, that is an interesting concept.

S2: (*written*) I think Absolute Monarch is not good for society. As Student 1 said, it is easy to control country to use Absolute Monarch, but in the Absolute Monarch only king or queen has absolute power of everything in the country. So other people never get control and only follow what the Monarch said. You can see a lot of Republic countries today because more people think that nation's leader should be decided by national people.

S3: (*written*) I agree with both Student 1 and Student 2 that I believe the absolutism can be a disadvantage for the countries. Monarchs could spend so much money on their luxury like Henry the Eighth. But there were some monarchs who had achieved awesome jobs, i.e. Frederick the Great who was the King of Prussia stopped the torture.

S2: (*written*) As Student 3 said, Henry the eighth spent so much money to show his power. People would be surprised and follow him, but I think people didn't want to see his power to use their money.

S4: (*written*) I believe that an Absolute Monarch could be bad for a society. While some absolute monarchs contributed to develop their countries suppressing all criticism to keep peaceful countries, most absolute monarchs just enjoyed their lives abusing their absolute power. As Student 3 said that there were some absolute monarchs who succeeded in controlling their countries. These monarchs suppressed people to maintain their power, for example, Tokugawa, Japan. Although Tokugawa absolutely controlled Japan in about 250 years, Japan in that period maintained peace, no wars. On the other hand, absolute monarchs abused their excessive power including using money for luxuries.

T: (*written*) Interesting. **Some questions for you all though**: 1. Are all the scandals going on in Japanese politics now with government officials accepting money or gifts to give out things OR charging the people for unnecessary expensive goods (sofas, trips, etc.) any different than an absolute monarch? 2. Would you want to live in Tokugawa Japan even though you think it was peaceful? Was it actually peaceful?

S2: (*written*) 1. I think, it is different because even if Japanese Government accepts money or gifts, the people in a government are chosen by voting, as for absolute monarch there is a leader who already decided and there were no choice for people. 2. I don't want to live in Tokugawa Japan, in that time positions were so different and important. Some high position people could test their knives by killing low position people.

T: (*written*) So, Student 2, **what you are saying that is OK or better to abuse your power if you are elected? You would prefer that?**

S2: (*written*) We cannot replace in the Absolute Monarch, but now we can replace. It is good for us! And have chance to vote and say in the Government.

As reflected in this example, the teacher engaged her students in active conversation using three strategies: 1) reformulating what the students said; 2) asking focus questions; and 3) stressing specific aspects in students' utterances. All of these strategies proved successful in engaging students in active thinking and responding.

Orchestrating interactions and synthetic thinking in the Ask A Question forum

Many teachers employ the technique of encouraging students to post their questions to a designated public thread called *Ask A Question*. This is often more useful than receiving questions from students by email and answering each student individually. Also, through this means, students become engaged in active negotiation of a problem and the collective search for a solution.

Example: Algebra (high school)

S1:   (*written*) For 6.5, #57, I don't understand where you plug $5×10^{-2}$ into. Are you supposed to plug it in as [H+]? And if so, then how do you solve it after that?

S2:   (*written*) yea . You do plug it into [H+] but then you have to turn it into logarithm form and then solve for the pH. i hope this helps. =]

S1:   (*written*) yeah it does... thanks :)

S3:   (*written*) how do you do numbers 54–59 odds on page 397?

S2:   (*written*) the hw on p. 397 is #13–35 odds, 36–47 all, 49–59 odd, 61–68 all, and 72–77 all

S4:   (*written*) That would include #54–59 odd that the other person was asking for. Lol

In such text-based asynchronous dialogues, certain students function as experts who master their own skills by providing answers and clues to help teach their peers.

Orchestrating interactions with reading partners

Assigning reading partners is another productive strategy to engage students in one-on-one interactions and synthetic thinking. The types of readings can range from fiction to scientific articles and from news to popular scientific readings.

Example: Reading partners (middle school)

Students assigned to read *By the Time You Read This I'll Be Dead* discussed the notion of suicide, a complicated and sensitive topic. The informal atmosphere of the asynchronous discussion allowed them to express their thoughts freely, saying what was on their minds. Such exchanges can be seen as contributing to the development of higher-order abstract thinking.

S1:   (*written*) I am fascinated in the book *By the Time You Read This I'll Be Dead*. The main character Daelyn has been humiliated many times and teased and bullied all the things nobody wants because of her appearance. Don't you just hate that... that people judge you? Well I do that gets me mad!! I read about so many bad things that had happened to her when she was small, and **I found that very sad, didn't you?** Okay I read that she goes to this website called 'ThroughTheLight.com' which has a counting if you... have an account of when you want to die. That was my OMG moment! **What was your OMG moment?** If you want me to speed up tell me okay?

S2:   (*written*) I actually really like it so far. **I think it's the best book we've read so far don't you?** The girl is so depressed I feel so bad for her. I would be so scared to leave her alone. She can't be trusted. If she would slit her wrists what would else would she do? Santana is a really nice boy and I think he can really help her and support her. If she would just let him inside her life he could really do a lot of things for her in a positive way. I don't think she hates her parents I just think she is embarrassed of them a little. That's nothing unusual for a teenager. **So just tell me what you think.**

S1: (*written*) That website that she continually goes on called through the light is kind of freaky **don't you think?** I would not go on there at all in my whole entire life. **Would you go on that website?** One day her parents are going to walk in on her harming herself. If that ever happens in the book I would be so shocked. Her parents are already worried about her enough doesn't she want to have some freedom? I would love to have freedom instead of my parents being on my back all the time. Obviously she doesn't want freedom so she go out and live a teenage life. That sucks for her really bad.

S2: (*written*) Well yeah it is freaky that she goes on that one website... who would have known there would be suicidal websites? There are many difficulties in a person's life isn't there? If not people are lucky. Isn't it cool that the kid Santana wants to be her friend? I find it very cute that he does and did he try to ask her out? **Do you like Santana should he be trusted with like Daelyn?** Because he doesn't seem like that type that wants to hurt or embarrass her. What else... oh do you like the book so far I love it, although it is really sad.

From the way these two students ask each other questions, share their opinions and seek clarifications, it is apparent that this type of online asynchronous conversation can be a tool for the development of critical thinking, especially because the affordances of this medium allow time to read, reflect and compose.

Orchestrating interactions and scaffolding synthetic thinking with text: section summary

Instructional conversation strategies that encourage student interactions with the target content and with one another are the meat of teaching with asynchronous text. Indeed, it is through these kinds of interactions that learners develop their ability to think deeply and express themselves concerning the material under study. The medium, the most widely used in online education, combined with a skillful instructor means powerful opportunities for learning and expression for learners of all ages.

Orchestrating interactions and scaffolding synthetic thinking in audio/video conferencing

Live instructional meetings have their own dynamic in terms of student–student interactions around content. These require careful preparation to ensure that, like in asynchronous contexts, learners can be properly guided to engage the content and one another in order to move toward synthetic thinking and expression. Like the face-to-face classroom, time constrains. Unlike the live classroom, each participant can be active and access as many resources as needed to comprehend and generate the utterances that are required by the live activity. An archive of the live session can also be made use of in subsequent planning, teaching and student review.

Orchestrating synthetic thinking

The dynamic hybrid of voice+text makes these *stimulating* environments in which synthetic thinking can be encouraged and supported through multiple modalities. These include students' aural and textual voices in recorded real time. Students can become active participants by creating a piece of knowledge to share, asking questions, providing comments and giving suggestions. The person who speaks orally becomes an accumulator of different ideas, thoughts and new directions while those who simultaneously express their thoughts in written form in the chat box become co-creators and co-shapers of a final product, be it a concept, an idea, details about some process and the like. In this lively, creative process of synthesizing a final product, students can be steered to articulate what they do using discipline-specific discourse. Moreover, knowledge is constructed in real time and is responded to immediately by students and teacher. As such, this process of synthesizing knowledge can occur without visible interruptions to the oral part in a chat box. While being non-disruptive, written questions, suggestions and ideas in the chat box can shape the flow of a disciplinary conversation in a powerful yet non-intrusive way.

Example: American history (middle school)

In this American history audio conferencing class, the teacher assembled students' questions and by answering them gave a student-directed lecture.

S1:   (*written*) I have a question. So, where was Jefferson in the penning of the **Constitution**?

T: (*oral*) Oooh, it's a good question. Sometimes this question usually comes up on the exam. Jefferson was in Paris. He wasn't there for the **Constitutional** signing whatso-ever. Jefferson was undergoing a severe depression. He was also extremely emotion-ally fragile, and they basically packed him up and sent him to Paris because you know his wife had recently died and as the result of that they wanted to get him out of the country to sort of bring his spirits back.

S2:   (*written*) um is it true that the fight to maintain **american independence** lasted until the war of 1812?

T: (*oral*) Ummm... Well... Basically we went to War – it actually called in many cases the second war for **American independence** because they basically felt that British were trying to sabotage **American government** through basically the alienation the **American trade** oversees and they were not recognizing **American rights**, right of America as **an independent nation**. That's why they went to war in 1812. It was pretty serious... So I would say it was true.

S3:   (*written*) just wanted to ask about something you mentioned earlier... why were there **differences between states**? like for example, over some issues, what makes some state alike and entirely different in point of view from the rest of the states?

T: (*oral*) Yes, they were basically **independent operators** for the most part. The states did not see themselves as a unified whole. So Virginia would argue with Maryland and New York would argue with New Jersey. So basically they were almost **separate countries**. And they were sort of arguing over financial futures, over river navigation, they were competing over the treaties of trades. They viewed the articles of **Consideration** as basically just a loose organization to protect themselves in times of war and they saw themselves as **independent operators**, not as **a united nation** at all.

S3:   (*written*) What cause two **states to be alike** in view, for example, New Jersey and Rhode Island and different from the point of view of Georgia?

T: (*oral*) Well, the main difference, Student 3, to a certain degree was that the small states wanted to organize themselves against the larger states. Also the smaller states tended to be in the North. The Northern states saw themselves, mainly from New Jersey and Pennsylvania up, I would say saw themselves differently than perhaps Southern states, Maryland down south to Georgia, mainly because of **slavery and agricultural differences**.

In spite of the lack of non-verbal cues (facial expressions and gestures), this teacher managed to maintain a class atmosphere in which students felt comfortable asking questions. They were the ones who corralled the teacher into using the target discourse that they wanted to focus on. Indeed, the students propelled the conversation forward by posing and responding to questions that related to the current discussion as well as to broader themes and larger ideas.

Example: Science fiction (high school and college)

In this example, the teacher skillfully orchestrated this multiparty conversation, a conversation that was happening both orally and in written form. By asking navigating questions, elaborating students' analogies, providing his own analogies and involving them in *comparative thinking*, this teacher created an environment in which each student contributed and thereby became a part of the synthesizing process (Figure 4.6).

T: (*oral*) I've got an impression from the reading that fantasy and speculation are the key to our future. We think how we look forward for the future and how it can be changed and how it may be built. So without that speculation about what our futures are, we can end up like these people from *The City of Ember*.

S1:   (*oral*) I like that connection between that novel and *The City of Ember* that you're making because that reminds me about that quote on page 29 on creating a believable speculative world. The elements of fantasy have to mash with the real world elements and be just as solid.

S2:   (*oral*) I agree. It has to be something you can envision.

S1:   (*oral*) I think I had a problem with *The City of Ember* at first. However, I used to watch *Logan's Run*. *Logan's Run* feels similar to *The City of Ember* except it was overpopulated and we had a giver releasing the people the age of 30.

T: (*oral*) Has anyone else read *Logan's Run*?

S3:   (*written*) no

S4:   (*written*) I have not.

Figure 4.6 Encouraging oral and written interactions in audio/video conferences

T: (*oral*) You're right. In that novel, *Logan's Run*, we have the same situation. Here is the society that unaware of the outside world and how they are coping by being in essence trapped in that cocoon. They can't burst the cocoon. They are quite satisfied with where they are. I think those kinds of novels like *The City of Ember* and *Logan's Run* make us think are we in the same situation but simply don't realize it? Are we so accepting of what's happening here that we cannot see that there are other options available so that we can actually escape what we're thinking the whole world is? Confusing, isn't it?

S1:   (*written*) The Matrix

S2:   (*oral*) Sounds like The Matrix.

T: (*oral*) Yes, it does. Think of the idea living under the illusion that everything is safe and would be protected when the essence was always in danger?

S2:   (*oral*) I think we all are like that. When we think about other countries and what's going on there I think some people think that it's not going to happen here. They say 'Oh, we're protected. We gonna be fine'. It's about being young. When you are young, you think nothing will ever happen to me.

S1:   (*written*) So does speculative fiction help students speculate about possibilities?

T: (*oral*) I think the great authors like Aldous Huxley of *The Brave New World* and George Orwell of the *Nineteen Eighty-Four* speculate how bad it can be if you are not careful.

S3:   (*written*) it makes you think

S3:   (*written*) because it opens up new opportunities.

S3:   (*written*) Some movies scare me because I think what if this does happen. For example like Transformers.

Encouraging comparisons and analogies and providing additional information on similar products, the teacher involved his students in active thinking and discussion of the various aspects of the phenomenon.

Example: Planting a tree (high school economics)

This is yet another example of an instructor stimulating students to pose questions to deepen and extend the class discussion (Figure 4.7).

Figure 4.7   Encouraging synthetic responses in audio/video conferences

T: (*orally*) The planting a tree starts with finding the right season. The right time to get started and you go down to the nursery and find something that looks kind of like this. This is a tree that got that its root ball is wrapped up in burlap there. You need to choose the time of a year and a place carefully. And there is a little bit of planning involved. So the first thing a later fall or an early spring is the only time you can plant. A tree needs to be dormant for a while.

S1:   (*written*) **Is it too late in the season now to plant a tree?**

T: (*orally*) **Is it too late in the season now to plant a tree?** No. It's pretty much any time when you can dig a hole. It's OK to plant a tree into the winter. You need to choose carefully where to plant the tree to avoid the other trees. You don't want to damage them. Likewise you don't want to have branches and leaves from the other trees.

S2:   (*written*) **How far apart should I plant?**

T: (*orally*) **How far apart should one plant?** It really depends on the size of a tree. You want to make sure that the tree has enough light.

S1:   (*written*) What's a good shade producing tree?

S3:   (*written*) How can you avoid tree roots come to the surface?

S2:   (*written*) Where do you get bone meal?

S1:   (*written*) Can you transplant trees within a few weeks of planting without irreparably damaging the roots?

S3:   (*written*) Should I plant grass up to the tree trunk?

S4:   (*written*) How do you keep the gypsy moths off the tree?

S4:   (*written*) How much water how many times a week?

S1:   (*written*) How can you tell if there are air pockets?

Breakout rooms

Some audio/video conferencing programs have a feature called **breakout rooms**. Teachers can divide students into groups and arrange them into several different virtual rooms within the same audio/video conferencing session. This feature allows for intensive and focused groupwork and pairwork.

Example: Project guess which celebrity? (middle school Latin)

This Latin teacher put her students in groups of four in several virtual breakout rooms with the assignment to select six famous people. For each person selected, students were to describe the person without using their name, and present their sentences to class. The class would then guess which person was described.

T: (*oral*) In your breakout rooms, make sure to listen to your group members as they say their sentences and give each other some constructive feedback. If they are talking too fast, tell them to slow down. If they are not talking loud enough, please tell them to speak louder so that you could hear them. Do you have any questions?

S1:   (*written*) wait so we need 6 people even though we are going to be making sentences describing them with 4 people

T: (*oral*) Yes. The other two are needed to make it difficult to guess.
        (*in the breakout room*)

S1:   (*oral*) I want to do Johnny Depp if you guys OK.

S2:   (*written*) I'll talk about Bieber.

S1:   (*written*) Wait, does Johnny have a wife? How's wife in Latin?

Breakout rooms are a great place for group collaboration and focused interactions. In this example, the focus is on vocabulary and grammatical structures.

Orchestrating interactions and scaffolding synthetic thinking with audio/video conferencing: section summary

Nothing beats the kind of adrenaline induced by real-time interactions. In the case of online conferencing, the excitement of fast-paced exchanges is heightened by the multiple, simultaneous modes of communicating that can be orchestrated. Students can interact with one another via the main, oral stream and/or at the same time use the on-screen chat feature. Such combinations can be used to encourage learner interactions using the focal content while encouraging the kinds of synthetic thinking germane to the subject area.

Orchestrating interactions and scaffolding synthetic thinking in text chats

By far the most popular mode of communication among contemporary young people, texting or text chats, can be readily adapted for instructional purposes to great effect. Student–student focused messaging can be orchestrated to steer learners to insight and synthesis while they are actively engaged in using the target subject area discourse. Like live audio and video conferencing, these interactions can be archived and used by both teachers and students to augment subsequent instruction, learning and synthesis.

Orchestrating interactions with experts

Live chat interactions with experts in a given field can serve as excellent means for involving students in authentic instructional conversations whereby they must comprehend and produce the language of the discipline. Moreover, pre-, while- and post-discussion work can be carried out via readily available internet resources that can be accessed on an as-needed basis.

Example: (Petro)chemicals – who needs them? (middle and high school)

http://www.petrochemistry.eu/

In this example, the teacher integrated a required text chat with an expert in the field of petrochemicals into the class assignment. As the topic clearly related to students' everyday lives, they eagerly participated in the discussion on the use of plastic bags and how this might be avoided (Figure 4.8).

P1:   (*written*) What should we – young students – do to eliminate polypropylene?

Ex: (*written*) I think it would be almost impossible! **PP** is everywhere and suited to so many applications. It is one of the most common **thermoplastics** used in everything from your car and computer to aircraft and sports equipment. But if you want to try to avoid it, check for the **PP** symbol on packages and bottles. You can visit a **chemical intelligence** website to see all the applications (www.icis.com/v2/chemicals/intelligence.aspx).

P2:   (*written*) When you were avoiding food packaging did you take into account how the food was transported to you. For example was it shipped in **plastic** crates?

Ex: (*written*) I didn't – fortunately – I just considered what was on the shelves in my local supermarket. But one of my colleagues, Elaine Burridge (you can google her), avoided food packaging and did consider how it was delivered. Again she found it very tough and got very hungry! In the past paper bags were common, or vegetables for example came unwrapped, and still local shops may provide unwrapped goods. But on the other hand, food wrap, such as **polyethylene**, helps to preserve food, keep it clean and is convenient.

(Petro)Chemicals – who needs them?

Chat activity

Guest: Andy Brice, Science journalist and Markets Editor at ICIS
Language: English
Age group: 10-20
Date: 20 January 2009
Time: 11.00 CET

Participating schools

France – Lycée Joliot-Curie, Rennes (Teacher: Michele Allier)
Germany – Tannenbusch-Gymnasium, Bonn (Teacher: Wolfgang Kehren)
Hungary – SEK Budapest International School (Teacher: Beata Jarosievitz)
Sweden – Buråsskolan, Göteborg (Teacher: Ingela Bursjöö)
Poland – Zespol Szkol Integracyjnych nr 1, Bialystok (Teacher: Malgorzata Zajaczkowska)
Poland – VI Liceum Ogolnoksztalcace, Katowice (Teacher: Leszek Jablonski)
Poland – I Liceum Ogolnoksztalcace im. M.Kopemika, Katowice (Teachers: Bozena Kubiak / Marek Goszczynski)
Poland – Zespół Szkół im.C.K. Norwida w Częstochowie (Teacher: Agnieszka Limbach-Sygiet)
Romania – School no.29 "Mihai Viteazul", Constanta (Teachers: Aurora Fagaras / Carmen Badea)
Romania – Colegiul Tehnic "Dorin Pavel", Alba Iulia (Teachers: Anghelina Ciotlos / Veronica Dur)

Figure 4.8   Orchestrating interactions in chats with experts

During such an authentic live chat, students not only receive expert answers to their questions but they are also encouraged to ask more questions by reading and referring to additional materials.

Assigning focus groups in chats

Chat focus groups are a great tool in developing students' analytical thinking skills while practicing subject-specific language.

Example: Intense exercise and the body (high school biology)

This teacher arranged students into focus groups with each group having a specific question to address. In order to provide a well-supported response, group members had to interact, exchange ideas and negotiate a final answer.

T: (*written*) During intense exercise, potassium tends to accumulate in the fluid surrounding muscle cells. What membrane protein helps muscle cells counteract this tendency? Explain your answer.

S1: (*written*) carrier proteins?

S2: (*written*) Lactic Acid

S3: (*written*) no, lactic acid is what is generated as a result of muscle movement, not a protein that helps block it. I dont know the real answer, but search google!

S2: (*written*) lactic acid is released to counteract potassium buildup in muscles, because intense exercise causes potassium to leak into the muscle area and disrupt function, causing fatigue. but re-reading showed me he's looking for a protein, so i dunno the answer is. lactic acid does counteract this though =D just isn't a protein

S4: (*written*) lactic acid is correct

S5: (*written*) it's a na++/k+ ion channel protein and lactic acid causes fatigue, it doesn't relieve it

In such chat focus groups, students not only actively interact with one another but also learn how to manage and compromise in their discussions. Such conversations also represent teachable moments for the instructor to push learners to think more about the issues they raise.

Orchestrating interactions with deep questions

Example: To Kill a Mockingbird (middle school)

http://mrgibbs.proboards.com/index.cgi?board=bird&action=display&thread=110

In the discussion about Miss Caroline Fisher in *To Kill a Mockingbird*, the teacher asked students questions that led them to ponder deeply in order to compose appropriate responses, responses that other students were eager to engage.

T: (*written*) Why do we meet Miss Caroline Fisher? How does she contribute to the story? What do we learn from the scenes she is in? Conversely, what might we NOT learn, or what might NOT happen if she were not included in the story?

S1: (*written*) i think mrs fisher represents the infiltration of new ideas from a more liberal viewpoint in a more conservative area

S2: (*written*) I agree. Miss Fisher is from a town with a different view point on the whole slavery thing. I don't know whether it is more conservative or not, it just has a different outlook on the way society should be.

S3: (*written*) The teacher is important because she gives a view from outside of Maycomb. We as humans only notice change... hot to cold, cold to colder, hot to hotter. From wherever the teacher lived, to coming into Maycomb and teaching was obviously different. Students there were most likely not allowed to tell the teacher information that she did not already know about, and they probably were not let along with going for a few hours on the first day of school and then leaving no matter who they were and what family they came from. In here i believe that i took that customs in new places that you have never been to is a sensitive matter and you need to listen and not talk and assume that your way is everyway and everywhere uses your way. If she was not in the story it would be like not knowing the differences between hot and cold.

S2:   (*written*) I don't think that the kids were not allowed to tell the teacher about the town, I just think that they are used to everyone knowing everything about the town, especially teachers, who from a first graders point of view know everything there is to know.

S4:   (*written*) yeah i agree to with Student 2... she has a different point of view and a different lifestyle (the cootie part with the boy). you can tell that she is not from your average hillbilly scene. you can first tell this from the scene where the cootie crawls out of little chucks hair and she flips out. she then makes him go home and use a specific shampoo and soap (i find that funny)... i also agree with trusting too about the social hierarchy system thing... u can for sure tell that they were grown up in different classes.

Orchestrating interactions and scaffolding synthetic thinking in text chats: section summary

Texting is a popular form of informal, recreational communication for a reason: it is quick, easy, controlled and enjoyable. When the topic of texting is instructional as we have seen in the preceding examples, these features are put to work in the service of instructional conversations between and among students, teachers and outside experts on a given topic or from a particular field. The potential of such a communication mode for stimulating and supporting lively interactions that lead to synthetic thinking cannot be overstated.

Conclusion

Contemporary education values active, minds-on learning. It is through dynamic forms of participation in the content and its attendant language that learners master the subject matter and ways of speaking, writing and knowing that serve them well academically and beyond. Designing, preparing for and orchestrating such interactions with the end goal of synthetic thinking through disciplinarily appropriate discourse is the challenge for online educators. As we have seen in this chapter's illustrations of orchestrating interactions and synthetic thinking, these steps and strategies are well worth the effort in terms of student enthusiasm, engagement and learning.

End-of-chapter activities

(1)   Google the term 'synthetic thinking'. Read at least three different definitions of the term. With synthetic thinking as the goal, design an online interactive activity that employs this chapter's instructional conversation strategies as part of its processes. What do you think might work well? Why?

(2)   Much of this text is about instructor 'orchestration' of learning online. This metaphor sees the instructor signaling students with a wand to perform. Come up with at

least two additional metaphors for what you see the instructor doing when teaching conversationally online.

(3) Explain to someone who knows little or nothing about online teaching and learning what it means to orchestrate online instructional conversations. Record your explanation. Review it and revise it so that it expertly captures your concept.

Further reading

Britt, M.A. and Aglinskas, C. (2002) Improving students' ability to identify and use source information. *Cognition and Instruction* 20 (4), 485–522.

Peirce, W. (2003) Strategies for teaching thinking and promoting intellectual development in online classes. In S. Reisman (ed.) *Electronic Learning Communities: Current Issues and Best Practices* (pp. 301–347). Greenwich, CT: Information Age Publishing.

Picciano, A. and Seaman, J. (2009) *K-12 Online Learning: A 2008 Follow-Up of the Survey of US School District Administrators.* Newbury Port, MA: Sloan Consortium.

References

Freeman, S., Eddy, S.L., McDonough, M., Smith, M.K., Okoroafor, N., Jordt, H. and Wenderoth, M.P. (2014) Active learning increases student performance in science, engineering, and mathematics. *Proceedings of the National Academy of Sciences* 111 (23), 8410–8415.

Picciano, A.G. (2002) Beyond student perceptions: Issues of interaction, presence, and performance in an online course. *Journal of Asynchronous Learning Networks* 6 (1), 21–40.

Saunders, W., Goldenberg, C. and Hamann, J. (1992) Instructional conversations beget instructional conversations. *Teaching and Teacher Education* 8 (2), 199–218.

5

Providing feedback in online teaching

In this chapter you will learn:

- the definition of providing feedback as an instructional conversation strategy;

- the special affordances of voicethreads, discussion forums, audio/video conferences and text-based chats for providing feedback;

- how providing feedback as an instructional conversation strategy can be undertaken in these online environments;

- how the environments' affordances can be taken advantage of to support and amplify this instructional conversation strategy.

About providing feedback

It goes without saying that when we converse, we expect our interlocutors to respond to what we say, be it via a noise, a gesture, a single word or a long statement or question. In the realm of instruction, it is the response that teachers and peers provide that often holds the key to negotiating the understanding of new material (Goldenberg, 2004). This form of response is often called feedback as it figuratively feeds back to the learner the salience the learner needs to make sense of what is being discussed. Tailoring such responses according to the larger instructional goals, target content, while honing in on what we know about group and individual learners, is much more easily accomplished in asynchronous online environments where all participants have the time and resources to compose (Meskill & Anthony, 2005). Synchronous online environments are more challenging in terms of the amount of feedback tailoring that can be accomplished; nonetheless, they have a trove of readily accessible resources for feeding back salience (Meskill & Anthony, 2014).

Providing feedback with voice

VoiceThread is particularly well suited for providing feedback. The recorded, asynchronous nature of this online environment means that students can attend to the same post as many times as they need, and rehearse and compose their own voice messages while editing as necessary. Moreover, feedback can be supported by appropriate links and files with detailed explanations, examples and clues. The advantage of this asynchronous communication format is that students can use these additional resources when it is convenient and they can spend as long as they need to reach full comprehension. Feedback can also include links to online learning objects to incorporate visual and aural elements. Finally, voice can provide a liveliness and punch to online learning experiences (Gillis *et al.*, 2012).

Corralling feedback

Teachers often provide feedback in small doses, gradually corralling students into the right place to meet the instructional goals of the course activity. This technique is particularly well suited to asynchronous voice environments where students have the opportunity to attend to the teacher's messages and to follow the teacher's leads.

Example: Foster's War, *book discussion (elementary school)*

Because communication in voicethreads does not happen in real time, students, especially at the elementary level, need teacher involvement in the discussion to keep them on track and establish the sense of a guiding presence. One effective way to accomplish this is to periodically summarize what students have mentioned in their oral postings and ask questions prompting them to elaborate. This is what the teacher in the following example does (Figure 5.1).

Figure 5.1   Corralling feedback in VoiceThread

T: (*oral*) In what way did the attack on Pearl Harbor change Foster's life?

S1:   (*oral*) It affected Foster's life in many ways. One of the ways was that his friend got taken away by the cops because he was a part of the Japanese Club.

S2:   (*oral*) Foster's life changed in that his Dad took part of the Silver War defense. Foster's Dad made Foster and his brother take pamphlets around to all the houses and make sure that they had black curtains to shot.

S3:   (*oral*) After the war, Foster's life changed because at school he had to start taking drills.

T: (*oral*) Foster's best friend was taken away like you stated because of his involvement with the Japanese group. His friend also could not come to school. Do you think this was fair? Can you think of another time in history where we had become afraid and treated a group of people poorly because of our fears?

S4:   (*oral*) Foster's father hated Japanese people. After the attack on Pearl Harbor he hated them so much that he smashed all the Japanese things made in their house except their mother's teapot.

S3:   (*oral*) No, I don't think it's fair because everyone should have a chance to go to school even if there is a war going on between their countries. Yes, I can think of another time in the Silver War because we were trying to treat blacks differently just because they were of a different color and we were scared that they might catch on us.

S4:   (*oral*) No, I do not think that was fair that his friend could not go to school. I think that the Cold War would be another example.

S1:   (*oral*) I do not think it would be fair because if everyone got to learn at least like math or any subject like that and their friends would just grow up to not know anything. That would be just really horrible. Another time we were afraid was just like really big part of it was slavery because whites were afraid of not getting any work done around their farms.

S2:   (*oral*) I don't think it was fair that Foster's friend could not come to school because then he would not know anything. He would have to take school all over again. Another time was when the Cold War happened.

Repetition is one of the forms that feedback can also take in oral modes. In addition to corralling feedback, the teacher in this example repeats or *recycles* students' utterances, thereby providing positive feedback. In addition, she establishes connections and strengthens students' sense of her guiding presence. Also, by asking the students whether the situations they described in their responses were fair or not, she prompted them to go beyond factual thinking and think on a more abstract and philosophical level. She also triggered their thinking about comparisons by asking them to provide similar historical examples. This type of feedback helps students keep focused on the topic and corrals them into employing reasoning to back their statements.

Peer assessment as explicit feedback

Peer feedback has long been considered a valuable strategy in traditional face-to-face classrooms. It can be nicely orchestrated in online classes as well. Once again, the asynchronous nature of the medium allows students the time to carefully craft their assessments while accessing resources as needed. By actively employing the new language of target concepts, those generating feedback are getting productive practice themselves as they model language for one another.

Example: Peer assessment of essays (middle school)

In this example, the teacher asked his students to comment on pieces of writing written by other students. He also added his own *explicit feedback* at the end (Figure 5.2).

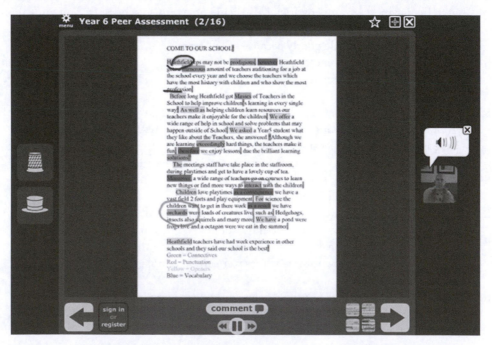

Figure 5.2 Peer assessment as explicit feedback in VoiceThread

S1:   (*oral*) I like the way this student has used really good words like auditioning, profession, and solutions (*circles the words on the slide*). One thing I caught is that she could previous the endings.

S2:   (*oral*) I liked the way this student used her openings in a good way (*circles the words on the slide*). This is a great word. Exceedingly. (*pause*) It's supposed to be a comma here (*writes a comma on the slide*). The first paragraph is supposed to be about children, not about teachers. Good connectives (*circles the words on the slide*). I could recommend these connectives to anyone.

T: (*oral*) OK, straight away on this piece of writing, I can see a good structure with the good paragraphs here (*takes paragraphs in brackets on the slide*). Inside the paragraphs, there are some very good vocabulary highlighted in blue: prodigious, numerous, masses, exceedingly, interact, orchards... all really well thought and add a lot to this style of writing. If we just look at the openings, how they vary, there is a very good range of openings which always keep things interesting for the reader (*circles the words on the slide*). On a range of punctuation, we've got commas, full stops, exclamation marks, apostrophe used correctly, space marks... Well done. Good piece of writing.

Through this peer feedback, both providers and receivers develop active fluency with the new concepts and their labels having practiced these actively in a meaningful context.

Implicit feedback

Because oral asynchronous environments allow for an unlimited amount of time for listening to and reading students' responses and to rehearse and compose instructional conversation strategies before applying them, feedback that contains implicit corrections, reformulations in more precise language of what students said can be powerful. Both students and teachers have the luxury of time to attend to their own and each other's utterances.

Example: Analysis of symbolism

In the following example, a student talked about her hopes but she did not use this specific term. The teacher summarized while using her intonation to lay stress on the target word. She elaborated on the student's thoughts, saturating her discourse with this word, and prompting the student to elaborate on the concept using the focal term (Figure 5.3).

S1:   (*written*) The Gentleman Caller symbolizes what the REAL world is like. Amanda, Tom, and Laura all live in a tiny isolated apartment where they created their own little worlds. And when Jim comes to visit them, it's like bringing the outside world into their house.

S2:   (*written*) The Gentleman Caller can represent the answer to everyone's problems; Tom's, Laura's, and Amanda's. The gentleman caller would provide financial security for Laura, which is what Tom needs so he can leave. The caller will also make Laura more socially acceptable, and make Amanda feel more at ease about her daughter; which solves Amanda's problems. And, although it may seem like Laura has no interest in a man, the caller would give Laura some confidence and a way to break out of her shell. And who knows, maybe he'll help her find love.

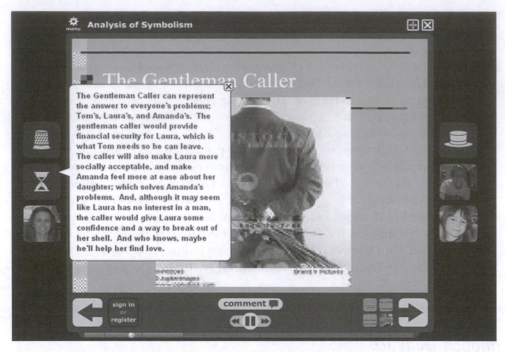

Figure 5.3 Implicit feedback in VoiceThread

T: (*oral*) Good points, Student 1 and Student 2! Also, I liked, Student 1, how you talked about the Gentleman Caller bringing a reality into the house and then, Student 2, you focused on how the Gentleman Caller brought some hope (*stressing intonation*) but I wonder ultimately what the implications that those hopes (*stressing intonation*) and dreams did not actually come true with this particular gentleman caller. Are all their hopes now dashed?

In her *implicit feedback,* this teacher gently refocused the student by stressing the key word for which she is seeking elaboration.

Collective feedback

A *collective feedback* strategy involves both insiders and outsiders commenting and providing suggestions within course discussions. This strategy can be easily implemented in asynchronous oral environments. Collective feedback can broaden students' horizons and let them engage the target content as it is in the wider world. By extending the readership of the coursework to those 'outside', content authenticity is augmented. Indeed, learning becomes participation in the discipline.

Example: Banned sites (middle school social studies)

In this example, art students post images that symbolize the banning of internet sites. They post these to a public voicethread that anyone can read and respond to. The variety of backgrounds of the responders made this collective feedback very powerful. Librarians, teachers, students, etc., took time to analyze these works and share their opinions (Figure 5.4).

Figure 5.4   Collective feedback in Voicethread

P1:   *(oral)* *(about first image)* I like this one very much, the one with the keyhole and the key that says Communication. And inside of the keyhole you see Creativity, Critical Thinking, Collaboration, Success, and Knowledge. It shows that when we block the Internet, we block it away from students. We're locking them away from something that is critical for their learning and their education. Lots of people don't under-stand why it's a bad thing. They think this is exactly what we're supposed to be doing – we're protecting students. And they don't realize how fallacious argument that is.

P2:   *(written)* *(about first image)* I couldn't agree more. I'm a high school student and I believe that limiting our web use limits our personal potential. Having unlimited access to the web has helped me become a more critical thinker and has introduced me to a much larger array of topics/subjects/issues that the news often censors.

P3:   *(written)* *(about first image)* I would like a little bit more color; the message is very clear from my point of view.

P4:   *(oral)* *(about second image)* I'm a librarian. I really like your image. The only thing that gives us feedback, however, is that my first impression would the lock dial connect to the internet images is that supposed to be that way? I have a hard time understand-ing from the graphic that you don't want to be that way. There is no message saying that locking the Internet is wrong or not the desired outcome. It looks like it's kind of supposed to be that way. So maybe I would rethink of ways of including something that lets us know as the viewers that you would prefer to be it unlocked somehow but I'm really enjoying this and think you did a great job.

Collective feedback composed of many diverse voices saturates students' internal repertoire with the target concepts leading to further development of their skills. Students are quite accustomed to using technology to produce and share their thinking on the internet. As this example illustrates, the same can be done with academic goals, processes and products in mind as well.

Anchoring feedback

In asynchronous voice environments where students and teachers are separated by time and location, it is crucial for the teacher to function as a discussion facilitator periodically summarizing and pointing out key ideas, highlighting target concepts, providing examples and important details, and suggestions for consideration and discussion. Anchoring such strategies to sources beyond the class can both focus and motivate learning.

Example: Alternative reality games (high school)

In a discussion about alternative reality games, the teacher provided feedback to the student's posting stressing his main points and making reference to (anchoring to) two outside sources (Figure 5.5).

Figure 5.5   Anchoring feedback in VoiceThread

S1:   (*oral*) I think it's interesting that people have found the way to take all these new electronic media that we have and all these new electronic ways of communicating with each other and turned them into the fun purpose, turned them into a game, for example, a detective game playing detectives with this technology. For me, a gaming is more of a solitaire activity when I want to play for an hour or two. I don't want to be in the situation that the first page describes when someone is going to call me at 3 o'clock in the morning and in a breathy tone tell me to stop pursuing whatever I'm pursuing. I think it's an interesting way to use these new tools that we have the way it's not really a tool but the thing is that we have all these people on the Internet doing these things when they probably could be doing something more effective. All these people are coming together to find someone who actually did not kill somebody whereas they could be coming together as people who actually create a positive change. It's waste of potential.

S2:   (*written*) I think you brought up a super interesting point in regards to, people could be spending their time solving REAL murders as opposed to fake ones. I mean, I do not know if that would hold up in our justice system but it definitely seems like something more worth people's time anyway. Maybe in the future people will be able to opt to have society solve the murder of their husband as opposed to the police... Another cool idea, what if politicians used ARG's to promote their campaigns? Eh? Ehhhh?

T: (*oral*) One book that springs to mind in a conversation with that Student 1 has posted here is the book by Clay Shirky called Cognitive Surplus. That book focuses on this notion that in the digital era we have more time and we can use that to do things or make things. He points to Wikipedia as the example of that. I read somewhere recently that world wide we have spent something like 100 times as much time playing angry birds as we have compiling entirely a Wikipedia. That's a bummer! (*written*) http://www.wikipedia.org

Such feedback conducted in a digital format in an asynchronous way can play a significant role in the process of learning as it allows for attending to referred items immediately as well as any time thereafter.

Providing feedback with voice: section summary

As we have seen, there are a number of instructional conversation strategies that work quite beautifully via recorded asynchronous voice. Teachable moments can be determined and a well-crafted response developed. Such feedback can be teacher and peer generated, explicit, implicit, collective and anchored to relevant supporting material. It can also be fashioned in such a way as to corral learners into comprehending and producing appropriate target content discourse. Voice has the added dimension of intonation rendering any of these instructional conversation strategies salient and engaging.

Providing feedback with text

Communicating asynchronously via text is by far the most common format for online instruction for any number of practical reasons. For educators it is a happy coincidence that feedback for learners in the form of static, yet malleable and archivable text is pedagogically powerful. Unlike the ethereal verbal feedback of the traditional, bricks-and-mortar classroom, feedback can be carefully developed in response to carefully considered teachable moments and, perhaps most importantly, can be re-read, reviewed and reconsidered as much as a student needs whenever and at whatever pace. These features render instructional conversations as tools par excellence for teaching and learning.

Providing explicit feedback

A great deal of teaching involves correcting students' errors, misinterpretations and misunderstandings. 'Explicit correction' is a term that can include a wide variety of instructional conversation strategies (Saunders *et al.*, 1992). These strategies not only aim to correct what students did wrong and get them on the right track, but also encourage them to think, develop skills for solving similar problems, see alternative points of view and develop facility with seeing the target content from a range of perspectives. In a traditional classroom, there are several scenarios whereby students react to explicit correction: (1) they may not notice it at all; (2) they may notice it but ignore it; (3) they may notice but not have enough time to interpret and incorporate it; or (4) they may misconstrue it. In written synchronous modes, corrective feedback has a reasonably good chance of being noticed and fewer chances of being ignored. Students have plenty of time to read and re-read teachers' comments and to think about the feedback provided. Moreover, students have the opportunity to ask more questions based on where the text feedback takes them. Written asynchronous environments provide more opportunities for individually tailored corrections when teachers can take into consideration students' personal characteristics and prior postings/learning and subsequently engage them in sustained dialogue around a topic of the student's interest and/or concern.

Example: Literature (middle school)

In the discussion forum called 'Comparing the Two Young Characters: Jessie v. Dara; Dara in The Clay Marble', the teacher, while praising her students' having found similarities between the two characters, explicitly directed them to find differences. To emphasize this instructional strategy, she uses the caps lock so that students will not overlook the feedback and her subsequent directions. One of the students immediately responded to this explicit request and elaborated on both the similarities and differences between the two characters.

T: (*written*) Both of our novels have centered around a teenage character that has gone through more than any person their age should go though. Jessie, was captured and taken away from his family to play his fife on a slave ship in the 17th century. His sole job was to keep the slaves 'dancing' as he played so they would remain strong on the long voyage to the Americas. Dara's life in The Clay Marble was turned upside down when the invading Khmer Rouge army destroyed much of her homeland of Cambodia. We have learned that almost inevitably, these young people with big hearts get taken advantage of and must resort to desperate measures during desperate times.

S1:   (*written*) I agree with this post about Jessie and Dara having a really hard time in their lives, moving or going to different part of the world

S2:   (*written*) i think they are totally awesome people that just kept going on in their life even when their lives are terrible. but they just keep toughing it up and kept moving

S3:   (*written*) I agree to. Jessie had to find his way home after a shipwreck with a slaves help and Dara had to find her family after a bombing with the help of her used-to-be enemy Chanay. They also each posses an item that comforts them. Jessie and his fife and Dara and her clay marble. They both experience losing their family and getting them back.

T: (*written*) GREAT POST! That's a great comparison between the two characters. I didn't even think about the two characters possessing something that has helped them in their difficult journeys. Well Done!

S4:   (*written*) I completely agree with the post. They both had to find their strength, they both had a comforting item, and (I can't exactly remember all of 'The Slave Dancer', correct me if I'm wrong) they both lost a friend that they met along the way. Another similarity I noticed is that they both lost their dads. There is a lot in common between these two, and they are both very kind characters in very good books.

T: (*written*) Great connection with the dads and the two characters. You guys are doing a great job comparing the two characters. ANY CONTRASTS OR DIFFERENCES??

S6: (*written*) These two books possessing two teenagers have a fair share of similarities and differences. In the Clay Marble, Dara is forced away from her beloved family, and in the Slave Dancer, Jessie is taken away from his mother and sister as well. They both lose their fathers in tragic ways and are left with a sibling and their mother. Dara is made to see horrible images such as gaunt children with missing limbs and bandaged bodies. Jessie is forced to see bone thin children and people and endure the terrible stench of vomit and human feces. Some differences are that although they both have things that comfort them, one is used to do something Jessie is against. Dara's clay marble only gives her strength and hope. Jessie loves his fife, but he has to play it in order to make the slaves 'dance'. This is something that Jessie is totally against. In the stories, they both meet good friends, and one that they will never see again. Jantu was a phenomenal friend, and she always will be to Dara, although her death causes them to never be reunited. Jessie befriends a slave, and they escape a sinking slave ship together, but the slave has to leave to find freedom, and Jessie may never know if the boy made it safely or not. They go their separate ways. In the end both teens find their family and make it home safely. Both find strength in themselves that they never knew they had, and leave a horrible past with more bravery, terrible images, and the memories of their old friends behind.

T: (*written*) FANTASTIC POST!! Well thought out and written. This is what I'm looking for from this 'Discussion Board'.

Explicit feedback visually enhanced by caps was effective in this case. It was combined with the teacher's commending of students' postings, thus doubling its attention-grabbing potential.

Example: Global warming...? – chemistry blog (middle school chemistry)

This is yet another example of explicit feedback where the teacher employs redirecting questions throughout the discussion. The teacher's explicit feedback helps students think outside the box, beyond mediocre ways of considering the content. She also deftly guides them to preview the outcomes of their actions. Her focus is on the development of students' ability to evaluate situations and consider consequences.

T: (*written*) Global Warming has been an issue for the world for some time. There has been strong support that global warming is an issue that is currently threatening to destroy our world as we know it (An Inconvenient Truth, Gore). There are also some that believe it is not global warming but rather global cooling (TIME). There are countless views as to this issue. It has even been a key issue in presidential debates in recent elections. It is the goal of this blog assignment to discuss the nature of global warming in our world. Is this an issue that we must deal with now? Is it even an issue at all? What can we do to attend to this issue? These are not the only questions, but you should form an answer that addresses these questions as well as any others that arise from the discussion. As this is a discussion, please read recent posts and do not repeat what has already been addressed.

S1:   (*written*) There are many things we can do to help prevent global warming this involves cars power plants and even our homes. When you program your thermostat in your home it cuts down on the amount of carbon dioxide released into the air. With your cars you can reduce the amount of carbon dioxide output by over 1500lbs. a year by walking, biking, or by taking public transportation. Another way to reduce the amount of carbon dioxide released into the air is by recycling. This can reduce the amount released by up to 850lbs. a year!

S2:   (*written*) There are a lot of more ways we can help to reduce the global warming. We could 'go green', which are small, simple things that make a difference in our world. We could conserve energy and electricity and switch to CFL bulbs. CFL bulbs use 60% less energy than normal bulbs and have a longer life time, which would obviously reduce electricity usage. We could also plant some more trees.

T: (*written*) Those are all excellent ways to reduce our 'carbon footprint'! But I think one thing a lot of people forget is the human element in all of this. How do you think people will really respond to these measures?

S3:   (*written*) There are a lot of more ways we can help to reduce the global warming. we could reduced the gas that we use so that people could have more money. they could use different ways a year by walking, biking, or by taking public transportation. people could help the environment by protecting the climate.

T: (*written*) So far we have opinions stating that global warming is going nowhere or that it is a natural process. We have even gotten recommendations on what we can do... but, how can we marshal forces to combat this? What does the public need to know about global warming? What is already being done?

The teacher reminds students to consider human factors when making choices and solutions, a critical skill for successful functioning in society.

Example: Chemistry discussion board. Questions before Exam 1

In this example, the chemistry teacher, in addition to providing the student with a direct answer to her question, encourages her to believe in her own skills and teaches her to be confident and independent in expressing her opinions.

S: (*written*) For Problem 123 on chapter 1, it asks for two answers, however the back of the book only gives one and the answer manual gives two. Also for question 77 in chapter 2 the answer in the back of the book does not match that of my own and the answer manual. Please advise?

T: (*written*) Yes, technically, there are two answers since two questions are asked. 2.77: The mass of Br-79 should be 78.92 amu. In general, don't get hung up so much on the answers as long as you understand how to apply the concepts. If your method makes sense, trust what you know and move on to the next problem.

Such individualized attention and coaching are facets of asynchronous text feedback that works well in diverse contexts.

Example: Animals in medical research

In this example, the teacher gently redirected the student to the original task of focusing on a specific research experiment. It is important to note that the asynchronous nature of the conversation means that valuable instructional time was not robbed from others by a single student's grandstanding, a feature of online learning that less vocal students laud.

S: (*written*) in my opinion, animal testing is cruel ...especially if the animal is alive. I have conducted research, and realized some of the horrible things that scientists do to achieve their goals. Some of these goals, however, are not very humane. Visit the site called http://www.all-creatures.org/wlalw/index.html and you will see the true story of how people in the medical labs treat their patients. A kitten with an electrode shoved through its head, how great is that? Everyone wants a pet with some sort of metal object jabbed through its cranium. If this is your type of pet, then go at it, but for me, ill stick with the cute fuzzy one that kisses your face. I'm out!!!! peace!!!

T: (*written*) OK, I think you may have lost a little of the point of your post by being extreme about the cat with the electrode. What was the purpose of the experiment? Do you believe that all laboratories are inhumane to their animals? If so, keep researching...

By this explicit comment containing key, target terminology such as 'the purpose of the experiment', 'laboratory study' and 'inhumane', the teacher corralled this student into discussing the assignment using appropriate discourse.

Example: Chapman 3D wire sculptures (elementary school art)

In her role as a discussion participant, a teacher can express her opinion using target terminology and target ways of speaking and writing about the subject. In this example, the teacher models the structure of a critique for her students. Using art-specific discourse elements such as 'focal point', 'compositional elements', 'flow of the design' and 'balance', she created a model structure for students to follow (Figure 5.6).

S1:   (*written*) I think this sculpture has really nice form and a strong use of color. The flower detail is a cute girly touch which I believe represents the artist very well.

S2:   (*written*) This is very messy... Just kidding, but seriously...

S3:   (*written*) This looks tight! you used great color.

S4:   (*written*) there's such an intense color. and movement.

S5:   (*written*) The idea is very cute and creative.... i think it could have been cleaned up some

T: (*written*) I think this sculpture does a good job with most of the compositional elements. I like the flow of the design, the unity by tying in the colors, and the balance of the flower with the ball at the top of the S shape. The one element that I see missing is the focal point. I think if more wire was added to the flower to make it stand out, it would be a lot better. As it is, your eye stays focused on the stand where the majority

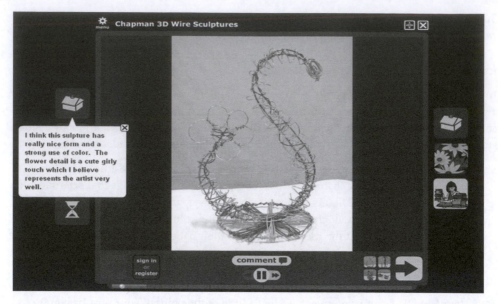

Figure 5.6 Feedback in discussion forums

of the wire is instead of continuing to follow on to what I think should be the focal point. Add more wire to the flower and you have a very nice sculpture.

S4: (*written*) The letter 'S' with flower accent can easily be identified within the sculpture. It almost looks like a living creature – maybe a snake or plant with vines. The sections of colored wire in the base help unify the bits of color running through the S-shape. I think the sculpture would really look nice in just copper and aluminum wire to make it more formal and cohesive. The inside of the 's' started out a bit messy, but you improved it. The loops around the S-shape could be more even in size to really make the craftsmanship good. Nice work.

While modeling appropriate subject-specific discourse, the teacher orchestrated the dialogue as a formal conversation about art rather than an informal exchange of opinions. Students picked up on her lead and began incorporating art-specific terms such as 'unify', 'formal' or 'cohesive' and used these productively in their own contributions.

Cluing as feedback

Cluing is a common technique used in a regular classroom. Providing hints and clues is a tried and true form of guiding learners to meet intended goals. The asynchronous nature of the medium allows for more time for students to pick up on the clues and react to them as the teacher intends.

Example: Lady Macbeth (middle school)

The teacher in the discussion about Lady Macbeth does not provide the right answers. She encourages her students to figure out the answers by giving them clues about where to look and what to think.

T: (*written*) 'We have scorched the snake, not killed it: She'll close and be herself, whilst our poor malice Remains in danger of her former tooth' (3.2.15-17). Here is our space to write up anything we know, infer or assume (we can correct ourselves as we go). What do we need to know about this quote? Think character motivations, literary devices, etc.

S1:   (*written*) Macbeth says this to Lady Macbeth saying though they have gotten this far by killing Duncan, Macbeth still hasn't gotten everything he needed to become king and all the bad things Macbeth has done will pretty much come back to bite him in the end

T: (*written*) What does this mean for the future of the play? What will this comment do to Lady Macbeth? Will Macbeth keep killing? What is controlling his decisions?

S2:   (*written*) I think Lady Macbeth is controlling his decisions. I think Macbeth will keep killing because of her.

S3:   (*written*) Macbeth is saying this to Lady Macbeth. He is saying how he did 'hurt Duncan' but, did literally kill him, he's saying he's not totally gone. What he did will come back to him and as Julia said it will 'bite Macbeth in the end'. There is danger to come of the cruel bloody action Macbeth did, that he will be threatened with. Macbeth is also saying Lady Macbeth will now be herself again because Macbeth did what she wanted him to do, but there will still be evil in her and Carma will come back to Macbeth.

T: (*written*) This quote is not about killing Duncan. Keep thinking... What could the 'snake' be?

S4:   (*written*) I think the quote is referring to Fleance as the snake. He might have damaged the future in the way he wanted but it is going come back to haunt him.

As we saw earlier, teachers can provide feedback by *recasting* what students say. Stressing some aspects of students' utterances and labeling main points with precise subject-specific terms, teachers can take students' words to a new level as in the following example.

Example: Student writing (middle and high school)

This teacher, in her feedback on the student's comments on another student's writing, labeled the writing technique that the student mentioned in her comments.

S: (*written*) I have taken a glance at CC's opinion piece and I think it was very outstanding. He gave many examples that described the meaning of the slogan and how he felt about it.

T: (*written*) So... giving examples seems to be a good technique for persuading someone... I would agree!

Helping students articulate precise definitions is important for their mastery of writing skills. Such knowledge guides review and revision processes and can serve as anchors when editing.

Corralling students into providing feedback

Example: Should Jackson be on the twenty? (seventh-grade, middle school)

In this example, the teacher developed a task that required his students to record 2–3 minute-long monologs in which they argue for or against Andrew Jackson's name appearing on the twenty-dollar bill. The second part of the task was to submit written comments on three randomly chosen peer monologs, outlining their strengths and weaknesses (Figure 5.7).

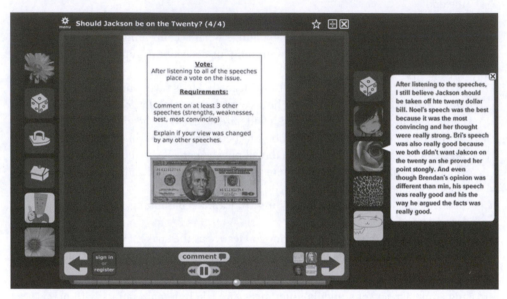

Figure 5.7   Corralling students into providing feedback

S1:   (*written*) I thought Audrey's speech was very good, especially the ending, but my one issue with it is how you were saying Jackson was making choices for himself, when he was actually making choices for his party, and the good of the people he favored. Nick's speech was fun to listen to, as usual, but no matter how many times you say 'trail of tears' my mind is going to remain unchanged. And finally, I think Noel's speech was great both because of its actually content and the conviction with which she presented it.

S2:   (*written*) I strongly agree with Tom and his decision about why Jackson should not be on the 20 dollar bill. Jackson was very suspicious when began his Presidency in office. He also took advantage of John Q. Adams idea of making his own cabinet with the people that supported him creating the Spoil Systems. When South Carolina wanted to secede from the states, he went to the extremes to taking control of the situation that even his VP had to leave. When he left the house he left with a lot of damages for the next President to clean up like Bush did with President Barack Obama.

As we can see, peer feedback can be powerful for both the recipient and the generator of the feedback. It can advance the conversation as well as validate learners' contributions.

Corralling outsiders into providing feedback

There is no question that with either online or face to face contexts, outside voices bring fresh and additive information and perspectives. This is especially straightforward to achieve in online asynchronous text environments.

Example: Express yourself

Here, the teacher created a voicethread in which students exchanged the poems they wrote based on the images provided. They posted these publicly in order to solicit comments from the wider online community. This extended the audience for their work to the entire world, a key consideration in the age of social media where broadcasting one's works and ideas on the internet is commonplace (Figures 5.8 and 5.9).

Figure 5.8 Corralling outsiders into providing feedback

P1:   (*written*) The emotion in your poem was so relatable to. I think that in middle school, many kids are forced to be someone that they don't want to be by their friends. You did a good job of making the reader feel the emotion in your piece. You used repetition and cool phrases like 'Sure I'll put that mask on, but that is anything but me'. The only weaknesses that I noticed in your poem were that you didn't use very many poetry techniques or interesting words. I also would like to suggest that you make your poem longer and that you have larger stanzas.

Figure 5.9   Corralling outsiders into providing feedback

P2:   (*written*) I really enjoyed your poem because of all of the emotion! My favorite lines were: 'he decides my future' and the line 'I hide in the dark'. Your poem really stands out because some people can connect to your poem! One line I think you could improve on was 'I am your shadow'. I would have made it 'I am a shadow'. I really enjoyed reading your poem!

Individuals outside of the class can freely provide input on students' work. In addition, they can provide definitions or links to important sources as in the following example.

Example: Global warming (middle school)

P1:   (*written*) Aw, poor bear. And yes, hunting polar bears is illegal in some places. Hunting illegally is called poaching.

P2:   (*written*) You can learn more about Spiral Island and Richie Sowa at http://spiralis-land.westkootenayunplugged.com/index.php.

Corralling students into structured feedback

Example: Photography (any level)

Involving students in providing feedback on one another's work can be structured with a task toolkit, a type of rubric as it is used here. In this example, the teacher created a template that the students were to follow in critiquing a photograph's strengths, what it expresses and any suggested improvements (Figure 5.10).

P1:   (*written*) S: the energy of the shot obvious, the movement I: You understand the use of color Im: get down to water level even more

P2:   (*written*) S: I can feel the movement of the water through the horizontal line theme I: Light play on water is beautiful. I: Perhaps a fill on that rock in the lower left third of the screen. This seems to be the anchor – could it have more prominence with more light?

P3:   (*written*) S: The black and white effects really gave it some depth. I: I really like how you can see all of the bubbles throughout the picture to add some detail. Im: Maybe move the rock in more of a corner so it follows the rule of thirds more.

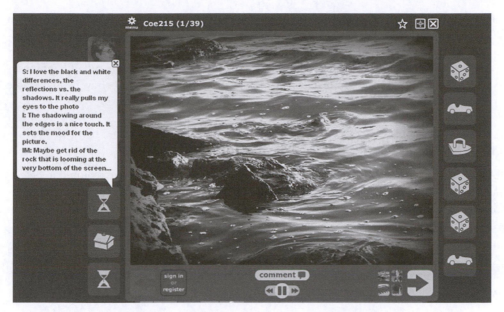

Figure 5.10   Corralling participants into structured feedback

Guided by the teacher-provided structured discourse, students used appropriate terminology and register rather than simply expressing their likes and dislikes.

Providing playful feedback

Playfulness in asynchronous written modes contributes a great deal to creating an atmosphere where students can discuss serious matters with ease and pleasure.

Example: Drawing lots

This is an example from a math discussion forum where one of the participants illustrated statistics principles in a playful manner when showing why an answer was wrong.

P1:   (*written*) Say a group of five people draw lots to decide which of them is to undertake an unpleasant task. Does the first person to take a straw have an advantage over the other four? My family is convinced this is so but I am not so sure. Their argument is that the first person to draw a lot has only a one in five chance of picking the short straw (the best odds of any round) and if he doesn't pick it then he is excluded from all further rounds. But in the first round the others are 100% certain not to pick the short straw while he is the only one taking a risk. The same situation applies in all further rounds. In each round drawing a straw incurs a risk that the others do not take but also offers the possibility of being excluded from further participation and risk in subsequent rounds. So do the benefits and risks of drawing in any round balance out so that there is no advantage in the long run of drawing the first, or any other, straw?

P2:   (*written*) The two events are not independent, because there is an expectation E(x) that the straw will or will not be picked in the second round. If we follow your reasoning, then every turn of drawing the straw is created equal and endowed by its Creator with certain inalienable rights, among which are life, liberty, and the pursuit of happiness. Would your expectation really be that the chance of drawing short straw is unalterable in every turn? Wasn't Disraeli who said it's easy to lie with statistics?

Providing feedback with text: section summary

Asynchronous text is a mechanism for feedback par excellence. The time required to detect teachable moments, then consider, develop and edit tailored feedback accordingly cannot be overstated in its importance as a pedagogical plus. We have seen how instructors can deftly tailor explicit feedback to guide learners' understandings and actions. We have also discussed ways that such feedback can be in the form of clues and labels. Finally, we have examined examples of corralling whereby instructors corral learners' online conversations, corral them into following a structured course in providing peer feedback and soliciting voices external to the course as a form of learning feedback.

Providing feedback in audio/ video conferencing

While asynchronous text feedback is an excellent instructional tool due to the amount of time afforded its generation and comprehension, there is nothing like the adrenaline of live human encounters. Real-time digital meetings can be lively and intense like the face-to-face classroom. Two aspects distinguish the environment in terms of feedback: (1) the numerous textual, visual and auditory resources that can be called upon and integrated into feedback; and (2) careful planning and orchestration on the part of the instructor. This means having at hand the kinds of resources that might become relevant during a live session that can be called up and incorporated as needed. In the following illustrations of live feedback, we will see some of this careful planning in play.

Summarizing and repetition as feedback

The audio conferencing mode of communication with its lack of visual cues, gestures and facial expressions, requires extra effort to keep everyone focused on the task and material at hand. Vocal and textual repetition and summarizing can be effective ways of helping students to attend and for the online conversation to maintain focus (Figure 5.11).

Example: Credit (high school principles of economics)

T: (*oral*) So those who use credit, it's imperative that if you are going to be the one who uses credit and I'm not advocating using it I'm not saying it's wrong or it's good I'm

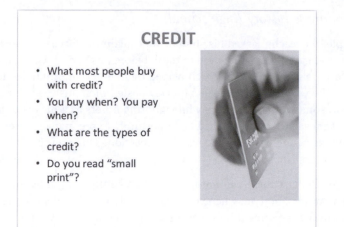

Figure 5.11 Summarizing and repetition as feedback in audio/video conferences

giving you an information, giving you an understanding of how it works because Americans use credit to pay for a lot of things. They use credits to buy their homes, to buy their automobiles, to make major purchases such as appliances or even travel. So if you are going to be in that statistics of people who use credit to purchase items like that, it would be very important for you to know how it works. OK, those are your notes to your activity that you should've done and I'm going to ask you questions just to make sure you guys are staying that you are on task. So first of all, the principles of credits. You buy blank, you pay blank. What should we answer to that, Student 1?

S1:   (*oral*) Buy now, pay later. Can I ask you about something? (*asks some logistical questions about the homework*)

T: (*oral*) (*responds to the questions about the homework*)

S2:   (*oral*) May I ask you something, too? (*asks some questions about the homework*)

T: (*oral*) So Student 1 has already responded to us. Credit is when you buy now and you pay later, OK? This is really important. Credit is not free money. Don't get to just borrow money and then never pay it back. You use it now and there will be expectations that you will pay it later. OK?

In this example, the teacher, as well as the students, were distracted by one of the students asking questions unrelated to the subject. The teacher provided positive feedback repeating what the previous student said and in doing so ensured their progress through the target materials.

Providing feedback with questions and clues

Teachers often steer students toward the right answers by asking them questions and giving them time to think and respond, then commenting on students' answers and refining their questions.

Example: Japanese history (high school)

In this example, the teacher asked his students to explain the difference between power and authority and gave them some time to think before answering. Using the chat feature of an audio conferencing program, which helped them entertain multiple answers that were visible to the whole group, students quickly posted their answers. The teacher commented on some of these answers while ignoring others as a means of providing neutral negative feedback. Students had an opportunity to see many answers and eliminate them as wrong based on the teacher's reaction. This prompted them to keep thinking about these two concepts.

T: (*oral*) We often use these two words – power and authority – interchangeably in ordinary conversation but when you're talking about political structures they are not necessarily are the same things. Let me ask you a question. What is the difference between power and authority?

S1:   (*written*) Power is real; authority is theoretical.

S2:   (*written*) authority 'given' by ones in power

S3:   (*written*) Power is military and authority is law.

T: (*oral*) Power is military and authority is law. Can be. But it can be broader than that. It can be... both can be civil as well. Both can be military. What else can you guys think?

S4:   (*written*) Authority is stated, power is a manifestation?

S5:   (*written*) Authority, the right to give command.

S6:   (*written*) Authority derives from consent, but power can enforce its self.

T: (*oral*) Authority is the right to give command. Authority derives from consent, but power can enforce its self. Let's see. Yeah. Really simple definition of authority is something that has power and ability to do it. Again, those are similar but not always exactly the same. You know very trivial kind of example. The state has the right to set speeding laws. It doesn't have power to enforce them. You don't have power to regulate citizens' behavior completely. In a broader sense we're talking about control of political mechanisms versus the legitimizing functions behind it. And those are always almost always separate. In the American sense, authority belongs to the electorate and sovereignty belongs to the people but power is still in the hands of the government. You can't turn around and say I choose not to pay my taxes because after all this is democracy and your right to make laws come in the first place. But it's different a little bit in Japan. We'll take a look at it in just a second.

Example: Algebra (middle school)

In this example, the teacher orchestrated the use of three online environments: synchronous oral, synchronous written (the chat feature in the audio conferencing software she used for her class) and asynchronous oral. In her lesson based on the game in which different cartoon characters made mathematical mistakes that students were supposed to correct, she used the first two listed modes to introduce and practice the topic by walking them through different stages of solving the problems. The choice of synchronous modes was well justified as students benefitted from the teacher's immediacy.

Preventing confusion and misinterpretations, being available for spontaneous questions and providing immediate feedback are the major reasons for selecting real-time modes of communication at the stage when a new topic is introduced.

T: (*oral*) Now here is where one of the properties comes in. So can you tell us what we need to do next with this problem? We need to get rid of that negative two. How do we do that?

S1:   (*oral*) You put it as a fraction.

T: (*oral*) OK, we gonna make the fraction. And now where should it go?

S1:   (*oral*) It will be one over two?

T: (*oral*) One over. OK. So now this is it. And let's get the law again. A to the negative N equals one over A to the N. OK? So here we have our one over. Now what is our base?

S1:   (*oral*) Negative one.

T: (*oral*) OK. Here is negative four. And what is the exponent going to be?

S1:   (*oral*) Two?

T: (*oral*) Two. OK. Very good. So now here we use that property of negative exponents. Now we still have to go one more step. So, Student 1, what is our final answer? (*pause*) One oveeeer? What's in the bottom? What is the denominator going to be?

S2:   (*written*) −2?

T: (*oral*) OK. Let's take a look at the denominator now? The denominator is negative four squares. So remember what that means? Negative four times negative four. So what is negative four times negative four?

S3:   (*written*) 16

T: (*oral*) Gooooood. Good-good. Sixteen. OK guys here is what George of the Jungles should have done.

In this conversation, both written and oral responses indicate uncertainness. Question marks and question-like intonation in statements indicate that students needed teacher guidance. Her immediacy in this regard is crucial to their learning.

The second part of the lesson was not intended to be done in real time. Students were asked to develop their own voicethreads containing their own 'criminal' math cases and comment on their peers' voicethreads. The teacher provided detailed oral and written instructions on how to use voiceboards and how she expected students to comment on one another's math stories.

T: (*written*) Prepare, create, and edit before publishing. Take your work seriously. Take your commenting seriously. Classroom rules apply – keep it 'G'. Be respectful.

This lesson is an excellent example of combining online modalities with the teacher orchestrating her feedback in the most effective way within each. There is little doubt that these students could in turn use the target algebraic vocabulary in their own voicethreads with a high degree of confidence.

Feedback by an expert

Audio conferencing is a great opportunity to bring different voices together to engage students in conversation with subject matter experts, thereby exposing them to the target discourse including specialized vocabulary.

Example: Music (high school)

In this instance, the teacher brought on board a musician and a music critic who could give her music students invaluable feedback on their compositions.

T: (*oral*) Welcome and we're back with our guest today talking about composition and learning more about how to fix the things that we've got started or general comments about things that he's seeing.

G: (*oral*) Hello! My pleasure. Hello you all virtual composers. Let's start up with Student 1. This is a piece that called Sketched. We are going to play it. Those who have access to his cords, follow up. (*piano playing*)

T: (*oral*) Nice job, Student 1!

G: (*oral*) One thing that is impressive to me is that the basic harmonic structure is so captivating that you can really go a long time without changing the basic tonal structure, the basic harmony. I mean you've got a two bar phrase with two harmonies in it and because of the instrumentation and because how interesting this idea is we can stay with it for a while before we really have to have a change. What we probably add to that point is that we should find somewhere else to go harmonically. The rhythmic idea is all the transitional idea. You have the piano at the bottom of the page six is great and I would be really ready for that. I think you can try even the section that goes a little further appeal harmonically. Even you keep the C as the base note, although I would practice changing it too, you could go somewhere else harmonically above it. I mean try using some B flat at times. I think you can use D major harmony.

This expert's feedback, delivered in a friendly and welcoming manner, is saturated with such area-specific vocabulary as 'harmony', 'instrumentation', 'rhythmic idea' and the like.

Explicit feedback to the group

Immediate and practically simultaneous feedback from one to many is something that is much needed in the lower grades and something that can be easily incorporated into audiographic conferencing.

Example: Algebra (middle school)

In this example, the teacher asked all her students to type their answers in the chat portion of the audio conferencing program so that she could easily and immediately attend to them and provide her feedback in a timely manner.

T: (*oral*) Type in what you think the answer would be for this problem. I want you to type in your exponential equitation for this problem and the problem again is that we start with a thousand dollars in the bank and the interest is (types on the slide) start with a $1000 in the bank.

S1: (*written*) y=1000X1.01x

T: (*oral*) Student 1, where is your exponent?

S1: (*written*) I can't do exponents

T: (*oral*) Use a little caret above your exponent. (*writes on the slide while saying aloud*) Interest rate is 1% per month. And everybody can see the Student 1 answer, can't you? Let's see if somebody can fix it and actually write it with the exponent and use a caret above the six.

S2: (*written*) y=1000*.01x

S3: (*written*) y=1000X1+.01^1

T: (*oral*) Here we go. Except, Student 3, you need some parentheses.

S3: (*written*) i mean 'x'

T: (*oral*) You need some parentheses, Student 3.

S3: (*written*) sorry.... i think

S4: (*written*) y=1000*(1.01^x)

T: (*oral*) Student 4, you are so close. So close! (*pause*) Anybody else would like to have a shot?

S2: (*written*) y=1000*.01^x

S1: (*written*) That's what I thought it was supposed to be.

S3: (*written*) y=1000(1.01^x)

S5: (*written*) y=1000 * 1.01^x

T: (*oral*) Nah... Not quite... It's OK. Student 5, you got it now.

S6: (*written*) y=1000*o.1^x'

T: (*oral*) Not quite, Student 6. Lots of you forget something. Let's go and talk about something. There are some good starts here. We gonna have (*writes on the slide and says aloud*) y=1000 * (1+.01)... (*provides an explanation*).

In this oral synchronous environment, the teacher was able to orchestrate peer feedback and interactions. She did so in a non-intrusive, nondisruptive manner whereby corrective remarks were typed into the chat box.

Providing feedback in audio/video conferencing: section summary

As we have seen, a number of instructional conversation strategies can be used to provide feedback in live audio/video conferencing. Strategies such as summarizing and repeating as a way to reinforce target content and corralling learning using questions and clues are particularly effective in this communication modality. Additionally, the literal voices of experts can be seamlessly integrated so that the subject area discourse is modeled and feedback from experts is received. Finally, audio/video conferencing is particularly well suited for providing specific, explicit feedback to the entire group at once while integrating the various modalities available.

Providing feedback in text chats

As we have seen, real-time chatting via text while audio/video conferencing can be very useful for providing feedback. What about outside of this aural and visual environment when communication is 'text only'? For individualized help in the form of feedback, text chatting is ideal.

Immediate one-on-one feedback

Chat provides opportunity for immediate one-on-one feedback if the chat session is scheduled during office hours or tutoring as in the following.

Example: Titration (high school chemistry)

T: (*written*) Find the number of moles of sodium carbonate in 20.0 mL of 0.500 mol L-1 solution.

S: (*written*) This is how i have tackled it but i am unsure if this is right.
        $n(Na2CO3)=cv$
        $=0.5 \times 0.02$
        $=0.01$ mol

T: (*written*) You don't need help on that question – that is the correct answer :) But there is another formula for doing this. Molarity equals to wt of $Na2CO3$ given divided by Molecular wt of $Na2CO3$ *Volume in ml divided by given volume

Providing feedback with references/anchors

One of the instructional conversation strategies that is particularly effective in text chat environments is providing feedback accompanied by anchors to the course materials or outside resources. There references can be added via an icon, a link made directly within the ongoing text-based conversation or as an embedded media file. This type of feedback is rendered more conspicuous in a fast-paced modality with the lines of chat entries moving quickly and participants concentrating on typing and reading at the same time.

Example: Dark matter (high school physics)

S: (*written*) it's said that it's present everywhere in the universe... does it possess mass?

T: (*written*) Not everywhere. Dark matter is matter which is not seen because they do not emit or reflect any detectable radiations or matter. Their presence is felt by gravity. Just like a blind finds that things are there by feeling it. It possesses mass and that is how it is felt.

S: (*written*) But it's not made of atoms... so how can it be influenced by gravity??

T: (*written*) Whatever be the elementary constituents, if there is matter there is gravity. Matter which cannot be detected, it may either be 100% absorbent or 100% transparent. In either case, its presence is not 'seen'.

S: *(written)* It constitutes about 90% of all substances in the universe... so it should possibly be present everywhere... even in our body.

T: *(written)* If you find any discrepancy between your observed mass and felt mass (inertia) then there is a possibility. Dark matter is not 'seen' because of the absence of any radiation from it. It has gravity. By the way who said 90%? It is not an easy task to explain everything via simple text chat. I recommend you go through the following links to understand dark matter and dark energy better.
http://science.nasa.gov/astrophysics/focus-areas/what-is-dark-energy/
http://imagine.gsfc.nasa.gov/docs/science/mysteries_l1/dark_energy.html
http://hubblesite.org/hubble_discoveries/dark_energy/

Feedback with redirecting questions

In the fast-paced environment of text-based chats, it is crucial that a teacher provide feedback as quickly and concisely as possible. Careful planning for such sessions is critical with as many resources as can be anticipated at the ready prior to the scheduled chat. Redirecting questions should be brief and clear so that students can easily pick up such conversational leads as in the following example.

Example: Cellular respiration

Having received unsatisfactory answers from his students who were unclear about what was being asked, this teacher immediately redirected using a brief question containing a key word. Students immediately responded to the clarified question.

T: *(written)* If there is a problem with the matrix working correctly. What will the outcome be?

S1:   *(written)* there will be no electron transport chain

S2:   *(written)* there would be no Krebs Cycle?

T: *(written)* what would happen to the individual?

S1:   *(written)* wouldnt be able to produce the atp

S2:   *(written)* no energy?

S3:   *(written)* would there not be enough energy

T: *(written)* you all have it correct

Providing feedback in text chats: section summary

While not particularly useful as a stand-alone venue for whole-class or even small-group instruction, text chats are ideal for individualized tutoring and/or pairwork. The two-way give and take is immediate yet re-readable and reviewable by participants. Instructional conversation strategies using redirecting questions to keep the student on the desired path and incorporating references and anchors as part of instructional feedback work well in chat modes.

Conclusion

When we take a conversational view of teaching and learning, the role of feedback cannot be overstated. It is within conversational turns between instructors and students and students and students that understanding and learning develop. The use of voice, text and any combination in online environments lends itself well to instructional feedback strategies that are part and parcel of subject area-focused conversations. The beauty of online feedback in contrast to face-to-face responses is that it can be more focused, more carefully considered and tightly tailored to learning the content.

End-of-chapter activities

(1) Choose one of the sample online conversations from this chapter. Generate a list of possible resources, referents and anchors that a teacher might hypothetically collect in advance of the online session to potentially assist and support the teaching.

(2) What kinds of 'outside voices' might you bring to your online instruction? Develop a brief protocol for inviting their participation in your course. Include a description of your goals and purposes.

(3) With a partner, brainstorm an online instructional conversation session on a decided topic. Come up with 'planned feedback' strategies that take the form of those discussed in this chapter.

Further reading

Gyabak, K., Ottenbreit-Leftwich, A. and Ray, J. (2015) Teachers using designerly thinking in K-12 online course design. *Journal of Online Learning Research* 1 (3), 253–274.

Rao, K. and Tanners, A. (2011) Curb cuts in cyberspace: Universal instructional design for online courses. *Journal of Postsecondary Education and Disability* 24 (3), 211–229.

Smith, J. and Dobson, E. (2009, October) Beyond the book: Using VoiceThread in language arts instruction. In T. Bastiaens *et al.* (eds) *E-Learn: World Conference on E-Learning in Corporate, Government, Healthcare, and Higher Education* (pp. 712–715). Chesapeake, VA: Association for the Advancement of Computing in Education (AACE).

Stover, K., Kissel, B., Wood, K. and Putman, M. (2015) Examining literacy teachers' perceptions of the use of VoiceThread in an elementary, middle school, and a high school classroom for enhancing instructional goals. *Literacy Research and Instruction* 54 (4), 341–362.

References

Gillis, A., Luthin, K., Parette, H.P. and Blum, C. (2012) Using VoiceThread to create meaningful receptive and expressive learning activities for young children. *Early Childhood Education Journal* 40 (4), 203–211.

Goldenberg, C.N. (2004) *Successful School Change: Creating Settings to Improve Teaching and Learning.* New York: Teachers College Press.

Meskill, C. and Anthony, N. (2005) Foreign language learning with CMC: Forms of online instructional discourse in a hybrid Russian Class. *System* 33 (1), 89–105.

Meskill, C. and Anthony, N. (2014) Synchronous polyfocality in new media/new learning: online Russian educators' instructional strategies. *System* 42, 177–188.

Saunders, W., Goldenberg, C. and Hamann, J. (1992) Instructional conversations beget instructional conversations. *Teaching and Teacher Education* 8 (2), 199–218.

6

Elements of effective online instructional conversations

Throughout this text, we have examined a great number of illustrations of online instructional conversations in action. We have placed particular emphasis on how conversation strategies are undertaken given different online venues and their particular affordances. In this chapter, we move in closer to examine instructional conversations from the perspective of the instructor, with recommendations and illustrations of more general teaching moves and their purposes that are effective in online venues. According to Goldenberg (1992), a founding instructional conversation theoretician, the anatomy of instructional conversations can be expressed in a model and with elements grouped by both *instructional* and *conversational* elements. We discuss and illustrate these two dimensions and *their* constituent elements as they happen in online and blended courses.

Instructional elements

Instructional element 1: focus on theme

As we have seen thus far throughout the text, effective online instructors carry on content-focused conversations, oftentimes thematically focused, with their students. That is, instructors have a specific content- and skills-specific plan in mind for their conversational focus throughout. They then steer learners' thinking and conversations accordingly. In effect, they have mapped out a plan or route they would like the conversation to follow that includes both big picture content (what learners will ultimately be responsible for in their assessments) and the smaller, moment-by-moment picture of how that content can best be intellectually engaged during a particular activity. This thematic mapping is something that experienced educators undertake as a matter of course, their deep fluency in the content and its discourse informing the broad picture and its component parts. Indeed, thematic mapping is also what traditionally organizes content in school curricula and textbooks (Figure 6.1).

Content mapping is an excellent organizing tool for developing both online content and as a foundation for planning, conducting and assessing the effectiveness of online

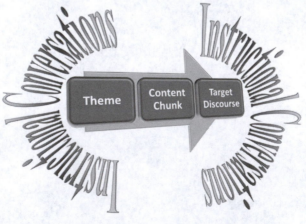

Figure 6.1   Thematic mapping

instructional conversations. This means that as content is envisioned and specified, so too are goals for student learning. Because a goal for all content areas is for learners to be fluent, both orally and in terms of literacy, in the language of the content and its attendant concepts, in developing thematic foci and the goals for each related chunk of content, a productive technique is to imagine the kinds of conversations you would like to hear your students actively and fluently participating in, conversations that would clearly indicate students' productive mastery of the content targeted. This envisioning of the conversation can serve a number of productive purposes. Indeed, if we look back to the illustrations of effective online instructional conversations throughout this text, we can reverse-engineer these to see what these instructors had imagined for their students as content mastery.

Each theme and content chunk within it then serves as a starting point to focus and guide the online conversation.

Example: Principles of economics (middle school)

In the following example, an economics teacher integrated several digital learning objects and communication venues in her lesson focusing on the theme of credit card use.

(*class announcement on the course website*)

T: (*written*) Yesterday, you did a lot of work on the concept of credit and how credit card companies prey upon young students. What you will do today is watch a film on credit cards and then participate in a discussion about them. Please after you have done your initial post replay to two of your classmates. To watch the video you will have to click here (*link*). Click here (*link*) for the questions that go along with the movie (the following questions were listed: What are five major causes of financial problems? What are warning signs of trouble? How much should we save? How long does information stay on your credit file?). When you are finished with the questions, place them in the Credit Movie Questions dropbox here (*link*). When you are done with the film, go to the following Discussion by clicking here (*link*).

(*audio conferencing portion of the lesson*)

T: (*oral*) What did you guys learn from the movie?

S1:   (*oral*) I've learned about the money transfer. When you change your different accounts, it's not making it better. It's just making it worse.

S2:   (*oral*) I've learned how easy it is to get caught on the money. I also learned that it's bad to consolidate your debt. Those store credit cards like Four Seasons... Like why it's bad to have them, how many credit cards you should have, what bankruptcy is... If you have a credit card, make sure you use it as a cash enabler basically. Is that what it was?

S3:   (*oral*) And I remember that as soon as the bill comes, you have to pay the whole amount to avoid paying an interest.

T: (*oral*) Those were good. Now I just want to go over the key points. Solicitations. What is the credit card solicitation?

S4:   (*oral*) Those are credit card applications that are coming in the mail.

T: (*oral*) Right. You got so many. Once you get like eighteen, you are going to be swarmed. You are being preapproved or you are being preselected... And those credit card companies are just dying to get you as a borrower.

During this audio conferencing lesson, the teacher discusses different types and systems of credit cards. While doing so, she also encourages her students to use the free online simulation called *It All Adds Up* available at http://www.italladdsup.org/mod1/. This online learning object can be used to teach credit card management techniques and helps students learn how to maintain a healthy credit card balance when making purchases and paying their bills. She thus focuses the instructional conversation on the theme of credit card use while providing multiple opportunities for learners to extend their content production and comprehension within the theme. Throughout her conversation, she uses the kinds of language attendant to credit and credit card literacy thus modeling the target language they need.

Mapped to the focal theme, this online lesson effectively combined activities to create opportunities for active learner participation in meaning making using the thematically targeted discourse of credit card usage. The instructor manipulated and arranged online resources (simulations, articles, images, videos, games, etc.) to stimulate and steer these processes. She crafted discussion questions and assignments accordingly. All of these activities and resources served the same goal: to investigate the topic through guided interaction in a range of communication venues.

Instructional element 2: activate and incorporate existing knowledge

Educators have long recognized the pedagogical value of tying what learners already know to new content; research uniformly supports this notion of connecting target content to existing knowledge and experience (Posner & Rudnitsky, 2001). Realizing connectivity between the target content and learners' extant knowledge base naturally requires that one has a good sense of who one's learners are, their educational as well as their outside-of-school backgrounds, interests and personalities. Getting to know students online has its challenges due most often to asynchronous contact with its absence of continuous visual and aural cues.

However, teaching online does have some advantages in this respect. First, the fact that instructors can continuously consult a running record of each learner's participation in online conversations, instructional and otherwise, represents a tremendously powerful tool. This includes a tool for gaining understanding of who learners are along with their interests and experiences, especially as these relate to the content area. So, for example, online instructors maintain student files that include the archived transcripts of course conversations along with the student's products and assessments. This provides a full picture of learners that can be consulted in the process of planning conversations and activities that connect the known and the unknown. Second, the ease with which connected texts, images and audio and video clips can be incorporated into instructional conversations, connections that can bridge to new learning from what is known, makes the online environment particularly practical when it comes to making such connections. Indeed, learners themselves can be asked to visually represent this kind of connectivity in their posts and assignments. Third, by having learners maintain a dynamic learning portfolio, records and representations of such connections can be documented by the students themselves as part of the learning process. The instructor can thereby consult individual students' portfolios as part of growing his or her own understanding of individual students' knowledge bases.

Students in online courses come from widely varied backgrounds in terms of socioeconomic status, ethnicity, orientation and the like. Therefore, bringing students' lived experiences into co-construction of meaning through instructional conversations makes perfect sense, especially in an environment where emotional and interpersonal risks are mitigated by the digital medium. Like for face-to-face (f2f) teaching, effective online instruction includes learning about and honoring students' stories. Based on dynamic, readily accessible information about students, online instructors make use of this information to hook learner knowledge and experience into the content and subsequently weave the known with the new. The following example illustrates an instructor taking what students already know and integrating this with the target content.

Example: Cells (high school biology)

During the audio conferencing portion of an online biology class, the teacher focused her students' attention on certain cell parts. She provided model descriptions for each of these parts. Afterward, the students, now equipped with the model descriptions, were redirected to the online resources she provided (interactive websites and YouTube videos) in order to find and describe other parts of cells that were not mentioned by the teacher. These students easily incorporated the terminology and concepts learned in this lesson as reflected in their own, original descriptions.

T: (*oral*) There are some other parts of cell like cilia which is a short little hair on the top of the little round and flagella which is also a long type of hair. Now I'm going to launch a web site. It's called the Virtual Cell Tour. I'd like you go to through that web site and I want you to come up with three different parts of cell than I haven't men-tioned and what they do and write it down on the interactive whiteboard. I'm giving you a couple of minutes to interact with that web site. I'm giving you some time to explore it on your own (*launches* http://www.ibiblio.org/virtualcell/tour/cell/cell.htm).

S1:   (*written*) ok, the Nucleus is basically the life of the cell. it keeps everything going and working properly

T: (*written*) Ok, good, thats 1 down

S2:   (*written*) the golgibody delivers the protein to the cell after the proteins are produced by the rough ER

T: (*written*) Ok, we like to call this the UPS of the cell, good, 2 of 3

S1:   (*written*) the Mitchondrian gives everything momentum and energy to work in the cell

T: (*written*) Great, its the powerhouse, 3 out of 3 (*oral*) OK, great job! Now we're going ahead and move on to the next part. The last section I'm going to talk about is how things move across the cell membrane. We have things called passive transport when stuff moves kind of on its own and things called active transport. I'm going to talk about this for a second and then I'm going to launch a youtube video here to get a better feel for you (*talks for a while and then launches* http://www.youtube.com/watch?v=0c8acUE9Itw&feature=related).

Through this entire activity, the teacher worked on guiding connections between students' existing knowledge and the new content-specific terminology and concepts they were learning. For example, she provided an analogy between the function of one of the cell's parts to deliver protein with United Parcel Service deliveries.

In asynchronous modes of online communication, activating and incorporating existing knowledge can be even more easily achieved as students have the luxury of time to reflect on what they have learned and undertake the necessary research to connect old and new knowledge. By actively filling in the missing pieces, they are learning to research and reflect.

Example: US history (middle school)

In this example, a history teacher assigned a discussion forum activity based on an oral class discussion, her lecture and course readings. Students were guided to think critically and come up with their own choices of what political party they would have supported if they had lived in the late 1700s.

T: (*written*) If you lived in the late 1700s, which political party (Democratic-Republicans or Federalists) do you think you would have aligned yourself with? Explain why. a. Use information discussed in class to support and defend your answer. b. You should have at least 2 key points to explain your choice. By the way, 'Having a nice wig' does not count! ☺

S1:   (*written*) I would most likely have been in the Democratic-Republican party because it was based on the fundamentals that the average American was smart enough to make decisions about his government as long as he is informed about the issue. This is good for me because I am living in the middle class and i am being raised to be independent, but also to be educated and informed about how people around me are doing things. And also because, I hate rich snobs, and that is the epitome of what Alexander Hamilton thought the people should be like that has control of our country.

S2:   (*written*) I would choose the democratic republicans because what is better than having ordinary people like you govern us and that they know what your interests are and think like you do. In the other hand the federalists are wealthy, educated people that know what they are doing but know what is best for their society not what is best for everyone else (poor, non-educated people).

The teacher directs the students to incorporate information they have recently encountered and playfully reminds them to stay within the bounds of serious speculation. Having learned in class that belonging to a certain socioeconomic class and one's educational background were key points in selecting a political party, these students successfully instantiated these concepts in developing a personal stance.

Instructional element 3: teach directly

As is often the case in the live classroom, it is often the case that direct explanations accompanied by comprehension checks are called for online. Indeed, in f2f classrooms, time constraints and attending to multiple students oftentimes lead to the use of direct teaching as a matter of expediency.

Example: Cellular respiration

Online synchronous written environments most closely resemble the f2f classroom as they are also fast paced and time constrained. Direct, quick, concise teaching is what students sometimes need if the written synchronous communication is conducted for the whole class or a large group. This is necessary to keep students involved and on task, just as in the bricks-and-mortar classroom.

S1:   (*written*) ok, i need clarification on fermentation. i answered the long question myself i just need to know when fermentation takes place

T: (*written*) Fermentation occurs when the body can't bring in enough oxygen.

S1:   (*written*) which is when glycolysis needs has no sugar?

T: (*written*) When there isn't enough oxygen the body performs anaerobic respiration which is fermentation. glycolysis always needs sugar

S2:   (*written*) anaerobic is not needing oxygen?

T: (*written*) correct Student 2

S1:   (*written*) when does glycolysis not have sugar?

T: (*written*) never Student 1

S1:   (*written*) ok then so when does oxygen take place

T: (*written*) It doesn't but for the next stage to occur it needs oxygen. if there isn't enough oxygen the 2 pyruvic acids go to fuel fermentation

S3:   (*written*) oh ok i got it now

T: (*written*) When there is enough oxygen the 2 pyruvates are changed into Acetyl CoA and that enters the krebs cycle

S1:   (*written*) so it goes 1; glycolysis 2; possibly fermentation 3; The kreb cycle 4; electron transport chain????????

T: (*written*) right Student 1

S1:   (*written*) ok glycolysis makes 2 atp actually 4 but it uses 2 as activation energy?

T: (*written*) correct Student 1

Unlike in the f2f classroom, providing this sort of on-demand, as-needed information becomes part of the running record. It is archived, referable and, therefore, salient to the learning of the moment and beyond.

Example: Algebra (middle school)

Audio conferencing classes are as dynamic and fast paced as the f2f environment. While it is always good to challenge students to figure out answers to their own questions, sometimes it makes more sense in terms of time and efficiency to provide short and precise answers and acknowledge students' correct answers directly.

T: (*types on the slide*) (0,2) (5,7) (*oral*) OK, each time you have the line like this, do you want to know the slope of the line or you somehow graph the line which has a slope?

S: (*written*) the slope

T: (*writes a formula*) (*oral*) OK, John, when you have a problem like this, do you know how to use formula?

S: (*written*) i think so

T: (*oral*) OK, let's say we have. (*writes on the slide*) Graph the line with a slope of 1 and a y-intercept of 2. (*oral*) OK, how about this? Is this what you were talking about?

S: (*written*) yes

T: (*oral*) OK, whenever you're graphing a line you are at the very least need to have a slope or you can have two points. whenever you have two points i give you 5,7 and 0,2. when you connect them you automatically have a line.

Example: Change for the better (middle school English)

In asynchronous online teaching forums, direct teaching is even less problematic and more effective as the venue allows for more thoughtful, tailored instructional conversation strategies to be considered and implemented.

S1:   (*written*) well now the first issue i would address is the war in the middle east, and helping the veterans for doing our 'dirty work'. i would like to see the government send an incomprehensible amount of military in. Then i want all soldiers past and present to be compensated for the service to their country...

T: (*written*) Thank you for your honest opinion Student 1! I have a feeling that you have a very strong opinion about this topic because of personal experience with a family member.

S2:   (*written*) In my personal opinion, i believe Health & Medicine should be priority number one in America. We have millions of people here in our own country living each day without health care that should be provided to all American citizens. In our neighboring country of Canada, health care is offered free to all Canadian citizens by its government, were as in our own fine country, our government is unable to fulfill the needs of it peoples medical issues. I believe if America were to establish a health care system like the one of our fellow Canada, it would resolve many of our issues and push forward to a better country and a better tomorrow for everyone.

T: (*written*) Wow! Great job class! I am especially impressed with Student 2's post and his stance on health care. Maybe we can be like our 'fellow Canadians' (Student 2's words...) someday. Then everyone would like hockey, too. That would be good.

As much time as needed can be invested in consulting and linking to other resources and including appropriate visual and aural material to amplify the language of direct teaching. In synchronous online formats, however, time and technical fluency constraints can make direct teaching a good option. In this case, anticipating the potential need for visual and aural accompaniments to such sessions is an important planning strategy.

Example: Colonial life (middle school history)

In this example, a history teacher used the online resource Advanced Placement US History Lesson on Colonial Life. This excellent multimedia presentation supplies both an oral lecture and a text version that help students visualize the past through images, listening to the lecture and referring to the text when necessary.

T: (*written*) LISTEN, READ AND TAKE NOTES from the HippoCampus.org link provided. (*link*) COLONIAL LIFE (*written*) Please confirm to me via a comment that you have completed your work. Let me know what you think of the materials offered.

S: (*written*) I found the material on the website to be somewhat insightful. The videos were full of information that gave me a closer look on colonial life. The readings, while lengthy, also had an abundance of facts. However, it is rather inconvenient that I have already taken the exam on this subject, for it would have been beneficial to study from this.

In both synchronous and asynchronous online forums, students themselves can undertake direct teaching by developing and delivering lectures, presentations, simulations or stories. Indeed, direct teaching from peers can be less face threatening and more comfortable for students than that from their teachers.

Example: Matrices lesson (middle school)

A student-recorded presentation in the form of a play teaches directly about matrices (Figure 6.2).

Figure 6.2   Direct peer teaching

S1:   (*oral*) Hey! I'm the matrices man.
S2:   (*oral*) And I'm super matrix. (*both*) And we're going to teach you about matrices.
S1:   (*oral*) What the heck is the matrix?
S2:   (*oral*) Matrix is a rectangular arrangement of numbers in rows and columns.

Instructional element 4: promote complex talk

Two hallmarks of online teaching and learning are (1) the level playing field online venues tend to represent and (2) the opportunities available for learners to share their thinking in multiple formats. Both open up possibilities for learning that are distinct from what can be achieved in f2f classrooms. When thoughtfully exploited, both can make online instruction superior to f2f classroom interaction for many students. First, the thinking time and resources that learners need is theirs to use as they see fit; consequently, instructors can be particularly demanding in this regard. They can construct and pose problems and questions for which they can expect learners to take just as much time as they need and for which learners can access as many assistive resources as they need to address these thoroughly and well. Learners otherwise constrained by time, space – both relational and physical – and access can enjoy optimal contexts as they develop their responses and products for their online instructor and classmates to review. This means the challenges, levels of complexity and their accompanying comprehension and articulation can be greatly ramped up. The second hallmark of online forums as regards the complexity of the content and the language needed to express this complexity is the medium itself: instead of paper and print, learning products can comprise multimedia in any combination, thus again complexifying the instructional conversations about the course content.

In terms of micro-level pedagogical strategies, online instructors can elicit more complex and extensive oral/written responses from learners by using techniques similar to those in a live classroom: e.g. *Tell me more about____* or *What do you mean by _____* or *Can you say that in a different way?* Clearly, the advantage that teachers have is the time and space they need to consider when and how to best employ such conversational techniques with learners who have the time and space to consider and construct refined and complex responses.

Example: Reading class (middle school)

In this example, the reading class teacher prompts her students to elaborate on their own contributions by posting the questions 'What do you think was the most...?,' 'What is evidence of...?' and 'What support can you find for...?'.

(*The Hunger Games Discussion Forum*)
S: (*written*) I have to say that the book is one of the best yet. It has intriguing thoughts and moments throughout it. I was very shocked at some events that occurred in the story. For those who have yet to reach the end I guarantee you will be pleased, but the real drama happens in the second volume, Catching Fire.
T: (*written*) What did you think was the most shocking or intriguing scene in Hunger Games??
(*The Crucible Discussion Forum*)
S: (*written*) I believe John Proctor is quite an interesting character in The Crucible. He is married to Elizabeth Proctor, but in love with Abigail. Although he is caught in this internal conflict he is still faithful to his wife by trying to stay away from Abigail. His wife doesn't go to church because of Abigail and Proctor's relationship and Proctor stays home with her to keep away from the temptation Abigail proposes. This dedication is quite noticeable throughout the beginning of the story.
T: (*written*) I find it interesting that you wrote John Proctor is in love with Abigail... do you believe that? If so, what evidence would you use to support it? I love your topic sentence. Do you think Abigail is more manipulative or more malevolent? Which can you find the most support for?

Example: Literature discussion: Tuck Everlasting (elementary school English)

Promoting complex talk is extremely effective in asynchronous online instruction when students cannot be immediately affected by the physical and verbal tone set in class by the teacher. Indeed, in asynchronous online modes, there is a greater risk of learners digressing and becoming involved in exchanging emotions rather than academic thoughts and ideas. The teacher reminds her students to become involved in complexly expressing their subject-specific thoughts and engaging concepts.

S1:   (*written*) I think that the stranger is Miles son because his son may still be alive because Miles drank out of the spring before he got married. Maybe, just maybe, his son has the same blood, like Miles and his beard is just gray because he dyed it so nobody would notice he hasn't aged his entire life.

S2:   (*written*) I love this book!

T: (*written*) Student 2: Why? Please make sure if you share your ideas you are specific so people can either extend on your comments or respectfully disagree with specific points.

Instructional element 5: require sources for statements and positions

Twenty-first-century educators recognize shifting sources of authoritative information (Kirk & MacDonald, 2001). The amount of online material that learners can access makes this particularly vexing: how does one sort through what is academically acceptable and endorsed versus information that is specious and/or inappropriate? In short, it has never been more important to teach otherwise digital savvy students what constitutes reliable and academically acceptable information to support their statements and positions, a key aspect of mastery of and fluency in a content area.

Contemporary students have the double responsibility to (1) determine the source and veracity of the information they wish to use in conversations and products in their courses; and (2) articulate the bases of these along with their use of the information to support the statements they make and the opinions they express. Promoting the former requires strategic, direct instruction and constant vigilance. Promoting the latter requires instructional conversation strategies that push learners to provide sources for the arguments they make. This can be accomplished by steering students to use authenticated online resources accompanied by solid, articulate reasoning when taking a position. Modeling and employing various probes to keep learners tuned into the imperative to supply support can take the form of statements such as 'How do you know?' 'What makes you think that?' 'Show us where it says __'.

Example: Greece (middle school geography)

Good teaching involves helping students to focus on details and providing more precise and accurate answers to the problems inherent in the content area. Modeling this as well as directing them using hints and other prompts works nicely in online venues (Figure 6.3).

S: (*written*) Here's my question˜ What could the Greek government have done more to save more people from the floods, perhaps predict it, or maybe, just maybe, prevent it? :)

S: (*written*) Answer for Question. I think that the Greek government can at least reduce the damage as much as possible when the flood had occur by constructing barriers like floodwalls or beams to prevent the water from entering into the buildings or blocking the drains of their houses, with installed sewer taps with appropriate check valves.

T: (*written*) Are you considering present or past Greece? Can you find more information about the effects of weather and climate on the Greek civilization of the past?

S: (*written*) http://www.historyforkids.org/learn/greeks/environment/greekweather.htm our question is, what could the ancient Greek government have done to minimize the damage caused by flood?

Example: Figurative language (middle school English)

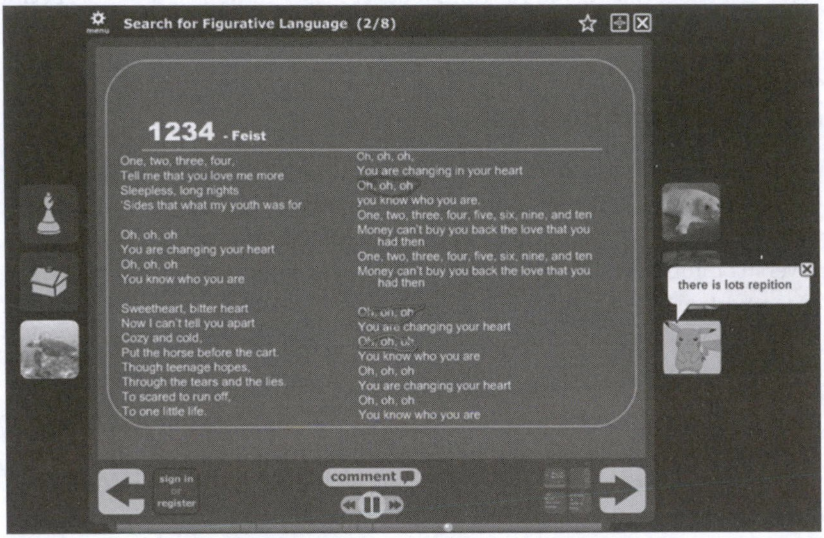

Figure 6.3   Asking for sources

S1:   (*written*) It uses lot of figurative language like when you say you're changing your heart, you don't really change your heart. You are not really changing your heart but like making new life better. Put the horse before the cart is really cool.

S2:   (*written*) this is repetition

S3:   (*written*) Metaphor

S4:   (*written*) there is lots repetition (*circles some examples*)

T: (*written*) Where is repetition and where is the metaphor and why?

Example: The Holocaust (middle school social studies)

Often, students themselves take the role of teacher and request explanations and sources of information for their classmates' statements and positions.

T: (*written*) How does something as big and terrible as the Holocaust happen? What forces are at work to enable one man to take control of a country and convince everyday ordinary people to go along with his plan for world domination and mass extermination of millions of people? Could it ever happen again?

S1:   (*written*) Something like the holocaust is a terrible thing that happened. This was caused by one person's hatred of another group of people. He thought that everyone else was different if they weren't pure Germans. Another reason for the holocaust was that people just followed their leader. Even though some may not have agreed they went along because their leader said it was the right thing to do. Some people probably didn't even know that Hitler was mass exterminating groups of people. As he rose to power he promised people that he would make a better community for Germans. I believe that is how he got people on his side.

S2:   (*written*) I think you should have said or explained whether or not you think the Holocaust will happen again or not.

S1:   (*written*) Just because we have cell phone and internet doesn't mean that something like that couldn't happen again it just means that it could be stopped faster. If it happened once, it can happen again.

S3:   (*written*) Student 2, I agree with what Student 1 says 100%!

Example: Sickle-cell anemia isn't half-bad! (high school biology)

The teacher sets the tone of an online conversation. In this example, the student contributing the initial response to the teacher is the second person in this chain whose post sets the standards for the subsequent discussion. The initial student's post contained sources of information as well as his own thoughts and questions for the rest of the group. It is apparent from this discussion that students had been instructed previously not only to provide online sources but also to evaluate them for their reliability.

S1:   (*posted an article on sickle-cell anemia*) (*written*) Confused? There's a whole lot of confusing vocabulary in this post. If you are, just check the source. It really accurately defines everything and helps you to understand the specifics. Can you find any other diseases or disorders that have this heterozygote advantage? Do you have any unanswered questions about this concept or any comments about the condition itself?

S2:   (*written*) According to my independent research, an example of another heterozygous advantage[https://www.hippocampus.org/] is Tay Sachs disease . This disease causes lipids and a fatty substance called ganglioside to build up in the brain's nerves and tissue cells. It is common among European Jews and in infants, who usually die by age four even with intense treatment. The horrible effects of Tay Sachs disease are becoming blind, deaf, and they are unable to swallow. After having the disease for a while paralysis takes place. People diagnosed with the disease also get red spots in their eyes. To tell if people have the disease a blood test is issued. In order to get the disease both your parents must have the mutation that causes the disease. Tay Sachs disease is considered a heterozygous advantage because it can aid in the prevention of Tuberculosis [http://www.news-medical.net/he...] If you want more information on the disease check out: https://en.wikipedia.org/wiki/Tay%E2%80%93Sachs_disease....

S3:   (*written*) Student 2 I will have to disagree with your information. When I did my research I found that Tay-Sachs disease may have advantages but it is not proven https://en.wikipedia.org/wiki/Tay%E2%80%93Sachs_disease

S2:   (*written*) Student 3: My first question to you is your resource credible? If your resource is credible it states that: 'Being a Tay-Sachs carrier may serve as a form of protection against tuberculosis. TB's prevalence in the European Jewish population was very high, in part because Jews were forced to live in crowded conditions. However, several statistical studies have demonstrated that grandparents of Tay-Sachs carriers (who are more likely to have been carriers themselves) died proportionally from the same causes as non-carriers'. [http://encyclopedia.stateunive...]

Example: Atoms and molecules (elementary physical science)

When online students exhibit difficulties answering a question and defending their position, the teacher can assist them by providing reliable electronic sources of information (Britt & Aglinskas, 2002).

S1:   (*written*) oh I get it now, it looks like molecules
T: (*written*) Cool, right? That is why it is called the ATOMium... atom, get it?
S2:   (*written*) its sugar
T: (*written*) Why do you think that, Student 2?
S3:   (*written*) idont think its a atom/molecule
T: (*written*) Why do you think that?
S4:   (*written*) im trying to search of what kind of atom it is. so far, there's no information about which atom it is.
T: (*written*) I added another link. (link to the YouTube video) Click on the picture of the Atomium to get there.
S5:   (*written*) It said online its a crystal molecule... a model of a crystal molecule
T: (*written*) Yes, it is a crystal. What type of crystal?

Conversational elements

Conversational element 1: avoid the 'known answer question'

Research on teaching and learning clearly underscores the futility of known answer questions as a teaching strategy (Cazden, 2001; Nystrand, 2006). Known answer or monologic questions are questions for which the poser of the question already knows the answer. Teachers often use known answer questions in live classrooms as a way of checking in with learners and as an expedient form of evaluation.

T: Which side of the road is the school on, North or South?
S: South.
T: Right.

As an instructional technique for teaching content, however, it is both inauthentic and ineffective. It breaks the fundamental rule of human conversation: questions are for finding out the unknown. In short, why ask a question if you already know the answer?

Instructional conversations whereby participants ask questions for which they *don't* know the answer, and for which there are conceivably any number of different answers, comprise a far more socially and cognitively engaging and realistic process (Tharp & Gallimore, 1988). Fortunately, in online venues, both instructors and students have the time and resources to develop and pose more open-ended and authentically interesting questions to explore as in the following.

Example: Julius Caesar: people's champion or evil dictator? (middle school social studies)

Controversial topics and complex historical figures whose roles in history can be interpreted from different perspectives can often initiate lively discussions especially when students are made to realize that their opinions are heard.

T: (*written*) Julius Caesar was assassinated by members of the Roman Senate on March 15, 44 B.C.E. Do you think that the senators were justified in their actions? Did Julius Caesar deserve to be assassinated, or was he a hero to the Roman people who should have remained in power? Answer the question with specific historical facts and examples to support your opinion. You must also respond to at least one other post, explaining why you agree or disagree with that person. To read an account of the assassination by an ancient Roman, visit http://www.eyewitnesstohistory.com/caesar2.htm.

S1:   (*written*) i think julius should not have been assassinated because even though he was cruel to some people he still did what was best for rome, so i think he was a champion for Rome

S2:   (*written*) i agree with Student 1 in that julius was the one thing that stop people from revolting and rome collapsing it kept them from dining earlier

S3:   (*written*) I disagree with Student 2 because Julius Caesar was a tyrant and also wanted to become king so he could have a family member take the throne after he died. Caesar also had no respect for the Roman Republic's Constitution. And treated the Senate as servants

Conversational element 2: respond to student contributions

While having an initial plan and maintaining the focus and coherence of an online discussion, teachers are also responsive to students' statements and the opportunities they provide. Again, the affordances of asynchronous online instruction in this regard cannot be overstated. Student contributions represent very powerful teachable moments when educators have the time and resources to consider and respond.

Example: Physical property (elementary school science)

In the following example, a science teacher successfully implemented several instructional conversation strategies in her initial post and in her responses to others. With the list of physical properties to be addressed, she corralled her students into filling in the blanks from her list using their own examples. Having observed her students not responding the way she had planned, she implemented modeling that the students in turn followed. She also acknowledged a student's response in a playful manner. Seeing her student digressing from the assigned topic, she gently but firmly guided him back on track while acknowledging his contributions. She corralled him into staying on-topic with topic-specific follow-up questions. This is an excellent example of instructional conversation strategies at work.

T: (*written*) At home, find one liquid or one solid to observe. Please describe as many physical properties as you can! Remember: Physical properties are anything that can be observed about an object by using your five senses. (Hint˜ you can and paste the list below to add to your comment!)
COLOR:
SHAPE:
SIZE:
TEXTURE:
TEMPERATURE:
HARDNESS:

S: (*written*) The color of a popsicle could be any color. It could be many sizes. It is the shape of the cup. It is hard and smooth. It is about 32 degrees and then it goes to room temperature. It is the flavor of a fruit.

T: (*written*) A great list of the physical properties of a Popsicle! Maybe you can find something in your house and give the physical properties of that. For example, in my house I found a cactus. Here are its properties.
COLOR: green
SHAPE: tall, cylindrical
SIZE: small
TEXTURE: smooth
TEMPERATURE: room temperature
HARDNESS: spongy
FLAVOR: –

S: (*written*) My new room is white, it is square, and it is about 15×12. The carpet is smooth and the walls are bumpy. It is room temperature. My room is hard on the walls and soft on the carpet. I am not going to lick everywhere in my room for the flavor.

T: (*written*) Thanks for a great post about the physical properties of your new room! Very clever! (I'm glad you don't know the flavor! :-)

Outsider: (*written*) I liked the part where you turned a liquid into a solid. It's almost like magic! But can you turn a solid into a liquid?

S: (*written*) You can freeze a liquid and then let it sit out for a while and then it is not frozen.

T: (*written*) You are correct! Heat will turn a solid back into a liquid. I like how you are commenting back to our readers. It's nice to end a comment with a question so you can get a conversation going in the comment section. However, it should stay on topic. For example, this topic is about matter... so here is a follow-up question for you. I'm wondering... if you put a cup of water in the freezer, does it freeze from the top down or from the bottom up?

S: (*written*) It fills top down because it reaches the top first.

The asynchronous mode of this discussion allowed this teacher to detect, think through and carefully craft her postings to maximize teaching and learning opportunities.

Conversational element 3: orchestrate connected discourse

Truly instructional conversation is characterized by multiple, engaged and connected turns both integrating and representative of the discourse of the content area. Recall that part of thematic mapping and instructional planning is to envision what kinds of academic conversation you feel would represent your students' best understanding of the content you have selected to focus on. It is then a matter of orchestrating, building on and guiding the complexification of that academic discourse in ways that lead to activation and deepening of student participation. Successively building on prior utterances and pushing learners to new insights are exemplified in the following.

Example: Stem-and-leaf plots (middle school math)

There are many different ways to engage students in connected discourse. Asking them to identify each other's difficulties and to try to resolve them together is one such technique represented in the following example.

T: (*written*) Read a classmate's blog about stem-and-leaf plots. Blog back an idea that might help them with the part they feel is difficult.

S1:   (*written*) some of my class mates said that a stem and leaf plot is about the mode median and the mean, but the stem and leaf plot is actually about getting data, putting the data in order least to greatest, and putting them on a table called a stem and leaf plot!

S2:   (*written*) Student 1, it easy to put the data in there when you put the data in the stem and leaf you cross out the data as you go

S3:   (*written*) Student 2, it is easy to put the data on the stem and leaf plot all you do is put the numbers on from least to greatest. if the numbers have the same tens number put them in the same row.

Example: Slaughterhouse-Five *book circle*

Using the technique of requesting, the teacher guides students to respond to their peers' postings. By corralling feedback, she inspires a thoughtful discussion with students making connections via the teacher's corralling strategies.

T: (*written*) Please have at least two members of your book circle comment here. You should report on the ideas your group discussed, as well as on the quality of your group process. In addition, at least two members of your book circle should visit the blogs of the other AP Lit classes and respond to their comments.

S1:   (*written*) My group discussed the anti-war aspect of the book and how Vonnegut expresses his anti-war views. We discussed the repetition of 'So it goes' and discussed why it is important that it is said whenever a death occurs. One question that puzzled us is whether Billy is Vonnegut and whether the narrator in the first chapter is Billy of Vonnegut. Another major topic of discussion we had is about the significance of the Trafalmadore's carrying their eyes in the hands.

S2:   (*written*) As Student 1 said we definitely delved into whether Billy Pilgrim is
        Vonnegut himself, but are uncertain. However, we also acknowledged that regardless
        of whether or not he is, names are extremely important. Beyond this, we also noted
        that there seems to be an almost anti-commercialism in Vonnegut's writing as he
        references Motor Cars, Coca-Cola and other well-known makers.
        We also discussed the complacency with which Billy Pilgrim seems to approach war
        and just moving through time and life as with, it would seem, the Trafalmadore's
        philosophy mixed in his story-telling. Furthermore, we mentioned that the war
        which Vonnegut describes does not contain many of the eager, dream-filled folks like
        Ronald Weary, but more often children and those hurled into it whether they like
        it or not regardless of how they appear to the other side. For example: the German
        Shepherd Princess. She's a farmer's dog.

S3:   (*written*) We also noticed the importance of the dog, who from a distance sounded
        terrifying, but when it came closer, it was just a farm dog named Princess. Things
        always seem to look different from different sides and angles, like war. Some see
        that children are being sent, some don't. I think this will also tie into the whole eye
        motif, how things are different and the importance of vision, both physically and
        mentally.

T: (*written*) I'm glad you're talking about the themes of the novel. I hope you also study
        its artistic elements. The book is rich, with quite a bit going on below the surface.
        Also, do you like the style?

S4:   (*written*) We also discussed the true identity of Billy Pilgrim. We decided it was
        Vonnegut because of the way very beginning of the book is written. The war's
        effects on the speaker's entire life are very evident and we believe that this is
        evidence of Vonnegut being the speaker. There was also talk of a possible eye
        motif, so we will focus on that. Our group is not particularly fond of Billy Pilgrim
        and the 'go-get-em' attitude he so greatly lacks. We are interested to see if he can
        redeem himself in our eyes later in the book. I think it is important to men-
        tion Vonnegut's dry humor (especially in the first chapter) which I particularly
        enjoyed. Vonnegut's stream of consciousness style also keeps things moving and
        interesting.

Example: Rosencrantz and Guildenstern are Dead (high school English)

Even though the word 'discussion' implies the exchange of opinions often in the form of
questions and answers equally and among many, students commonly make it a priority to
answer questions posted by their teacher. An effective discussion technique is to remind
students to ask each other questions as well as provide their own opinions as modeled by
the teacher here.

T: (*written*) Discuss similarities and differences you notice, and also think about the
        characters of Rosencrantz and Guildenstern. Are they interchangeable – two sides
        of the same character? What about that coin flipping? What might that represent?
        Happy discussing! – oh, and feel free to add your own questions and insights as you
        think of them.

S1: (*written*) While reading, i found myself trying to determine what the coin toss-
     ing could have represented. When you first flip a coin you stare at the face that is
     upright; however you never realize what it can look like on the other side. Just like
     people, society, and even the characters in this story. People don't ever just take a step
     back and realize how everything has two sides, they see what they want to see and
     nothing else.

S2: (*written*) I think the coin tossing represented the characters of Rosencrantz and
     Guildenstern. They seemed to be the same person at times (kind of how there are
     two sides to every person; one more logic and reasonable than the other). The two-
     faced coin represents the two sides to every person. since they were 'foils' of one
     another, they complimented each other's characters.

S3: (*written*) I still don't really understand all this coin flipping business, I just noticed
     that Ros caught Guil lying about it being heads to the Player. I'm not sure if that had
     any significance, it was just one thing I noticed.

S4: (*written*) Same here. I noticed that and I figured it meant something. Anyone have an
     idea?

S5: (*written*) this coin flipping kinda does show they are interchangeable and kinda
     shows them as one. like the saying two heads are better than one. bothros and guil
     posses very different qualities that when combined can become... something power-
     ful? maybe powerful. idk... but i think the two sides of the coin could mean that.

S4: (*written*) that makes sense

Conversational element 4: challenge playfully

We have seen a number of examples of instructor playfulness throughout the text. It seems
a natural aspect of online instructional conversations for this sort of balance between the
seriousness of the academic content and the varying perspectives, including humorous,
that one can bring to that content (Anthony, 2013; Çelik & Gündoğdu, 2016; Goodboy *et al.*,
2015). Modeling and encouraging 'the serious playful' is an instructional conversation par
excellence. A positive, non-threatening atmosphere tends to lead to more open, risk-free
exchanges in online courses (Bennett, 2008). This does not mean, however, that students
should not be continually challenged. Indeed, because the medium mediates affect, the
potential for students to experience challenges comfortably increases especially when the
instructor works to establish and maintain an atmosphere of mutual respect and trust to
build students' confidence in engaging the academic content (Figure 6.4).

Example: Chemistry, significant figures (high school)

In this blog, a chemistry teacher combined different online educational resources to grab
students' attention and to make the material challenging and fun. YouTube videos, tutorials
and simulations added to the story she wrote, making this lesson vivid and engaging.

T: (*written*) A group of Civil Engineers were at a conference being held in Central
     Australia. As part of the conference entertainment, they were taken on a tour of the

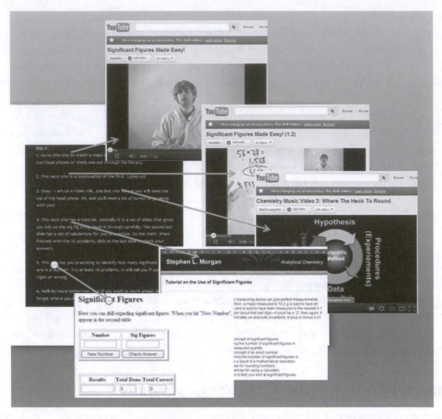

Figure 6.4   Conversational element 4: challenge playfully

famous rock, Uluru. 'This rock', announced the guide, 'is 50,000,004 years old!' The engineers – always impressed by precision in measurement – were astounded. 'How do you know the age of the rock so precisely?' asked one in the group. 'Easy!' came the reply. 'When I first came here, they told me is was 50 million years old. I've been working here for four years now'. I hope you enjoyed the significance of the joke I provided for you... if not, the original 50 million is an estimated value – 50,000,000 does not have 8 significant digits. Now for some activities for you to do with sig figs. We are going to be in the computer lab for 2 class periods. I have these activities/sites set up so that you will utilize each class period. Oh – one more thing. There will be a quiz given at the end of this session. Be prepared.

Day 1:

1. Go to this site (*link*) to watch a video on sig figs. Be sure to have your own head phones or check one out through the library. 2. This next site (*link*) is a continuation of the first. Listen on! 3. Okay – I am on a video roll... one last site (*link*) where you will need the use of the head phone. Oh, and you'll need a bit of humor to go along with you! 4. This next site (*link*) has a tutorial... basically it is a set of slides that gives you info on the sig fig thing. Read it through carefully. The second last slide has a set of calculations for you to practice. Do the math. When finished with the 12 problems,

click to the last slide to check your answers. 5. This site (*link*) has you practicing to identify how many significant digits are in a number. Try at least 15 problems. It will tell you if you are right or wrong. 6. We'll do more tomorrow... but if you want to work ahead, don't forget where you left off.

This lesson, conducted as a story of a group of civil engineers getting together during a conference in Australia, teaches students about significant figures in a playful manner. Adding different online resources helps students see the topic from different angles and observe subject-specific discourse in different contexts. Presenting complex matters in a playful context helps students connect these concepts naturally and effortlessly.

Example: Creative algebraic age problems

The use of humor can make even the most serious academic discourse comprehensible and engaging as in this voicethread portion of an algebra class (Figure 6.5).

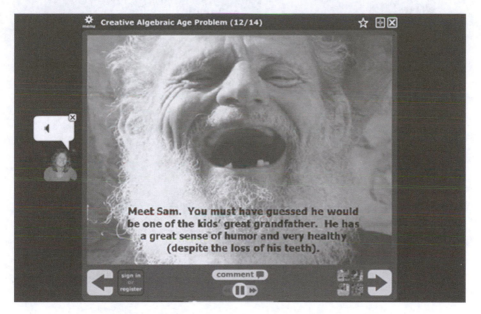

Figure 6.5   Conversational element 4: challenge playfully

T: (*oral*) In this problem, you name it according to some theme which I picked as age. You create a poem to go with your theme and then work on a challenging a complex problem that you create for the others to solve. Throughout your presentation, as you see in this model. You show how to exactly solve your problem. Show your representations and in the end come up with some creative additions to it. (*last slide*) This is the best character. Meet Sam. You must have guessed he would be one of the kids great grandfather. He's 92. Pretty old, hu? But he has a great sense of humor and he is very healthy despite the loss of just a few of his teeth.

Humor can encourage alternative perspectives and increase students' ability to create associations. It can ease learners into comparing and drawing analogies between complex material and everyday life.

Example: Physical and chemical properties

Self-deprecating humor can serve two goals: (a) instructional, when humor is used to illustrate the subject, and (b) non-instructional, when humor is used as an ice breaker. The following is an example of self-deprecating humor from an online physics class session that aimed to illustrate the nature of physical properties and physical changes (Figure 6.6).

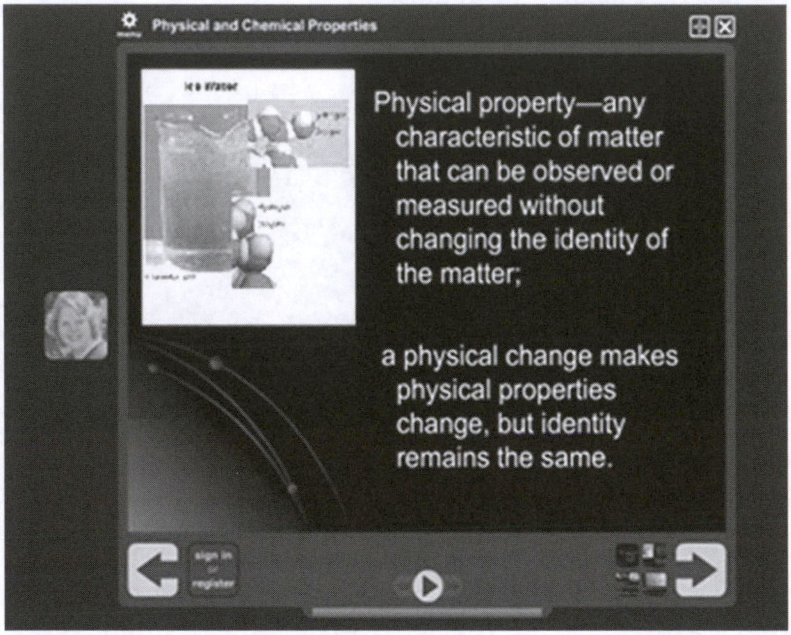

Figure 6.6   Conversational element 4: challenge playfully

T: (*oral*) A physical property is any characteristic of matter that can be observed – And a physical change makes physical properties change but identity remains the same, for example, if I lose a hundred pounds and have a collagen injection in my lips, I'm still not Angelina Jolie. I'm still Missis C. It's only a physical change.

This teacher achieved her objective – to show the essence of a physical change – in a playful manner. The image she used will surely stick in students' minds.

Online playfulness and playful teachable/learnable moments happen naturally. Texting is one of the most frequently used communication modes among children and young adults. Contemporary students are quite accustomed to making jokes and teasing each other at a distance. Such playfulness can be part of virtual classes and used as a learning tool.

Example: Project guess which celebrity? (middle school Latin)

This excerpt is from the text chat portion of a live class conducted via audio conferencing. It shows students' engagement in the subject and their desire to remain on-topic playfully when their teacher's microphone malfunctioned.

S1:   (*written*) u werebrutus too!!!!!

S2:   (*written*) I was BRUteee... Teacher, are you talking? we can't hear you if you are

S3:   (*written*) oh romeo oh romeo where for art thoromeo

S2:   (*written*) I will be brute when I want to jill :P you conspirator against caesar!

A creative teacher will always find ways to playfully challenge her students and make learning active and engaging (dialogic) as opposed to tedious lectures or student presentations (monologic). The following two examples illustrate how the use of humor and technologically enhanced play affects students' learning processes.

Example: Biographies of famous people (fourth grade)

In this example, a teacher asked her students to create presentations about famous people using Voki as a part of her wikispace-based class assignment (Figure 6.7).

Figure 6.7   Conversational element 4: challenge playfully

S1:   (*oral*) My name is Ben Franklin. I lived to be 84 years old. I was a printer, a scientist, and an inventor. I was born in Boston, Massachusetts. I've worked on my kite in the thunderstorm, a very dangerous thing to do, to prove that lightening was electricity. I also helped write the Declaration of Independence. I like to study and read a lot. I taught myself how to swim by reading.

S2:   (*oral*) My name is Abraham Lincoln. I lived to be 56 years old. I was President for March 4, 1861 through April 5, 1865. I was a lawyer. I served as a member of the US House of Representatives. I led the Silver War. I'm honest. I'm trustworthy. I'm dedicated. I'm loyal. And my nickname was Honored Abe. I was dedicated to the proposition that all men were created equally. All slaves should be free.

S3:   (*oral*) My name is Pocahontas. I lived to be 22 years old. I was first Indian to marry a white man.

Engaging in such educational play is important for child development. This personification of historical figures gives students a better, more intimate sense of historically significant facts.

Example: Spiders (elementary school, first grade)

Students used the website http://blabberize.com/ to animate their own drawings of spiders and give online presentations about them in a playful manner (Figure 6.8).

Figure 6.8   Conversational element 4: challenge playfully

S1:   (*oral*) I'm a spider. I'm black and I can build a web. I have a baby spider. Her name is Anna. I have eight legs and I have eight eyes, too. My body has two parts. I eat and drink water. I eat other spiders sometimes.

S2:   (*oral*) I'm a goliath spider. I have two body parts. I make silk. I hear and taste with my legs. I carry babies on my back. I have claws. I have six eyes. I have eight spinnerets. I'm hairy. I cannot see well. I'm the biggest spider in the world.

The moving mouths of these spiders create an illusion of live action helping students to make the characteristics of these species more vital, immediate and light-hearted.

Summary

These essential elements of instructional conversation strategies are a good place to begin in conceptualizing and designing online courses and online components to courses. They can also serve as useful heuristics to consider before, during and after conducting online activities. Reviewing transcripts of instructional conversations with these elements in mind is a helpful practice to polish your game.

Troubleshooting

If evidence of student mastery of specific content/concepts is not finding its way into students' posts, there are some strategies to try:

(1) evaluation of posts according to a rubric specifying what content/concept articulation is required;

(2) student development and presentation of products (multimedia presentations) that represent their understanding of specific content/concepts;

(3) requirement for student self-evaluations whereby they collect and annotate postings and products that demonstrate their mastery of specified content/concepts.

End-of-chapter activities

(1) Review the first example under the category 'Conversational element 2: respond to student contributions'. Come up with three strategies that could further enhance this instructional conversation. What are some strategies for determining students' prior knowledge on a given topic? How might these work in the various online venues? To best effect?

(2) With a classmate, colleague or friend, role play an asynchronous instructional conversation. Have your partner refuse to engage in instructionally appropriate ways so that you can try out the strategies listed. Cue your partner when he or she should change tactics.

Further reading

Bennett, W.L. (ed.) (2008) *Civic Life Online: Learning How Digital Media can Engage Youth*. Cambridge, MA: MIT Press.

Booth-Butterfield, M. and Wanzer, M.B. (2010) Humor and communication in instructional contexts: Goal-oriented communication. In D.L. Fassett and J.T. Warren (eds) *The SAGE Handbook of Communication and Instruction* (pp. 221–239). Los Angeles, CA: Sage.

Garner, R.L. (2006) Humor in pedagogy: How ha-ha can lead to aha! *College Teaching* 54, 177–180.

Jewitt, C. (2008) Multimodality and literacy in school classrooms. *Review of Research in Education* 32, 241–267.

Kozma, R. (2003) The material features of multiple representations and their cognitive and social affordances for science understanding. *Learning and Instruction* 13, 205–226.

Picciano, A.G., Seaman, J., Shea, P. and Swan, K. (2012) Examining the extent and nature of online learning in American K-12 education: The research initiatives of the Alfred P. Sloan Foundation. *The Internet and Higher Education* 15 (2), 127–135.

References

Anthony, N. (2013) Perceptions of humour in oral synchronous online environments. In C. Meskill (ed.) *Online Teaching and Learning: Sociocultural Perspectives* (pp. 157–175). London: Bloomsbury Publishing.

Bennett, W.L. (ed.) (2008) *Civic Life Online: Learning How Digital Media can Engage Youth*. Cambridge, MA: MIT Press.

Britt, M.A. and Aglinskas, C. (2002) Improving students' ability to identify and use source information. *Cognition and Instruction* 20 (4), 485–522.

Cazden, C.B. (2001) *The Language of Teaching and Learning*. Portsmouth, NH: Heinemann.

Çelik, B. and Gündoğdu, K. (2016) The effect of using **humor** and concept cartoons in high **school** ICT lesson on students' achievement, retention, attitude and anxiety. *Computers & Education* 103, 144–157.

Goldenberg, C. (1992) Instructional conversations: Promoting comprehension through discussion. *The Reading Teacher* 46 (4), 316–326.

Goodboy, A., Booth-Butterfield, M., Bolkan, S. and Griffin, D. (2015) The role of instructor h**umor** and students' educational orientations in student learning, extra effort, participation, and out-of-class communication. *Communication Quarterly* 63 (1), 44–61.

Kirk, D. and MacDonald, D. (2001) Teacher voice and ownership of curriculum change. *Journal of Curriculum Studies* 33 (5), 551–567.

Nystrand, M. (2006) Research on the role of classroom discourse as it affects reading comprehension. *Research in the Teaching of English* 40, 392–412.

Posner, G. J. & Rudnitsky, A.N. (2001). Course Design. Addison Wesley Longman, Inc.

Tharp, R. and Gallimore, R. (1988) *Rousing Minds to Life: Teaching, Learning and Schooling in Social Context*. New York: Cambridge University Press.

Tharp, R.G. and Gallimore, R. (1991) The Instructional Conversation: Teaching and Learning in Social Activity. Research Report: 2. Washington, DC: National Center for Research on Cultural Diversity and Second Language Learning.

7

Future directions for online teaching and learning

It is through others that we develop into ourselves. (Lev Vygotsky)

What do we believe we now know about effective online teaching and learning with young people? How can these new understandings help steer positive future policies and practices? Throughout this text, we have seen examples of contemporary educators making the most of online instructional conversation opportunities. The learning power and richness of these interactions are palpable. We have examined active, engaged learning in and for the 21st century, the design for which optimally combines the surfeit of opportunities and affordances given the internet and instructors' pedagogical prowess. We've seen online instruction that

- uses the medium as a platform for *all* expertise;

- extends conversations to embrace a range of perspectives;

- engages young minds actively, interactively and productively;

- is authentic in its communicative intent;

- is accessible to all;

- represents equal opportunity for all to participate fully and actively;

- maintains felicitous and productive communication about the subject at hand.

These characteristics grow out of instructor craft and finesse, especially in the art of instructional conversations. As more instruction gets augmented by and/or moved to online venues, these characteristics and their genesis must remain foremost in school policy and practice. The image of blank-faced, disenchanted children in front of banks of computer screens having been directed to interact with automated content – a much too frequent scenario in US schools in the last decades – comes to mind (Stallard & Cocker, 2014). By contrast, what could be more social and enlivening than entering a classroom full of chattering peers, taking a seat and participating in carefully focused and well-orchestrated conversations led by a talented instructor? Minus the sensations attendant to physical reality, logging on to a well-designed online course is no less vibrant with more opportunities for direct student involvement than in face-to-face. In addition to peers and instructors, students enjoy independent time and space to invest in these social–instructional exchanges at their own pace, in their own time, with access to infinite resources. This means that online courses can be more engaging and certainly more socially equitable than their face to face counterparts where students' natural enthusiasm can wilt under the tyranny of more aggressive students monopolizing the conversation (Meskill, 2002; Yukselturk & Bulut, 2009). In online venues where the playing field is level, learning can become fully participatory for all.

Moving forward

From 15th-century records, we know of an illness prevalent among cloistered clergy, monks and nuns who had taken an oath to spend their days in silent solitude and religious contemplation. The disease, labeled *acedia*, was also known as *the noonday demon.* This illness, or unseen force, caused people's attention to stray and disrupted the concentration so essential to religious contemplation. This same condition, it is now being argued, plagues young ***digital natives*** whose ways of being and understanding the world have been heavily shaped by the technologies they so widely use (Swingle, 2016). It is hypothesized that too much, too frenetic and too constant, hyper visual, aural and textual information is impeding attention, focus and thought. However, too little, as was the case with 15th-century religious devotees, can also lead to mental drift. Indeed, without other people present, without human conversation, human connection, both the overloaded and underloaded can stray from focusing on their work. By the same token, we know too well how underloaded and unmotivating the monologues of uninspired, disenfranchised educators can be. Simple human presence is far from sufficient. Skilled pedagogy remains the key to effective online learning (Picciano *et al.*, 2012).

In recent years, the educational community has come to recognize that learners and learning are far from generic as was once the prevailing foundation of many educational theories, curricula and methodologies. Learners are now recognized as complex individuals with intricate social and cultural histories, histories that shape the ways they see the world, communicate with others and learn. Likewise, contemporary instructors operate according to rich systems of understanding their craft, their learners, their subject areas and their goals. Classrooms are thus relational spaces where the complexities of human interaction serve to further knowledge and understanding (Noddings, 2003). In bricks-and-mortar schools, teaching and learning are constrained by this space and its limited resources as well as the time allotted for instruction. In online environments, by contrast, access to resources is instantaneous, supporting information and tools are limitless and opportunities for learners to interact intelligently with target content and readily converse about it are orchestrated by skillful teachers.

With contemporary learners taking so readily to social and recreational life online and coming to formal schooling equipped with accompanying digital literacy and multimodal habits of mind, as these new dispositions encounter traditional text-based, teacher-centered practices, we believe the former must cede to the latter. Not surprisingly, teachers are finding that when they take into account learners' digital expertise, they can more readily engage students in the work of school and achieve their instructional goals and way beyond. The many illustrations of excellent online instructional conversations in this text attest to this trend.

The future is the conversation

Historically, it has been the teacher-centered lecture and test paradigm, clearly the least effective way for children to learn and thrive, that has prevailed in education. By tradition, real classrooms are restricted spaces. In spite of all indications that learning is best achieved when there is active engagement with lively, authentic conversation in the language of the subject matter, teacher-centeredness or transmission education has evolved as a matter of efficiency. Sadly, this method has made its way into online formats. It is by far the least effortful and, consequently, intentional form of instruction imaginable. It is also the least desirable for learners, especially those who are otherwise pleasurably engaged online for recreational purposes.

Fortunately, as we have seen throughout this text, instructors are capitalizing on the social/interactional characteristic of today's digital fluencies to push and develop their thinking, understanding and active articulation of what they are learning. Whether future students will be learning via robotic, handheld, wearable or implanted technologies, the force that will remain constant is the power of talented human instructional processes: teaching by excellent teachers.

The following traits are modeled by excellent teachers and enacted in their work. They are dimensions of being social in educational contexts, online or off:

- curiosity and reverence for others and their worlds;

- accessing, using and generating knowledge responsibly;

- greater importance placed on the freshness and solidity of ideas rather than the thin and quirky;

- a sensitivity to the backgrounds and experiences of others when interacting;

- intelligent bonding of content in ways that are dynamic and historically reactive;

- a cautious and critical eye on the forces and agendas behind commercial interests;

- an eye to our essential selves that exist beyond the barrage of media banality and fabrications;

- social and intellectual generosity.

Efforts by those who wish to profit financially from a manufactured illusion of technology as a panacea need to understand this elemental distinction: devices don't teach, teachers teach. As we have seen, moreover, digital devices do represent a number of affordances for powerful instructional conversations.

Conclusion

Along with the speeding up of daily life due to new mobile technologies and their ubiquitous information comes responsibility on our part as we find ourselves constantly doing more. As educators, we have an obligation to learners to also *be* more. Understanding the human role and its complexities in the online learning equation is an excellent move in that direction. In a culture more often defined by self-promotion, branding and glitz, the need for educator grounding and intellect enacted via instructional conversations has never been greater.

End-of-chapter activities

(1) Take a look at the list of social/educational responsibilities presented. What do you think about such responsibilities for teachers? For students? For others? Can you add to this list?

(2) Have you ever taken a course, either online or face-to-face, that was *not* conversational? With a partner, brainstorm how that course might have been more conversational. What strategies might the instructor incorporate to encourage instructional interchange with the material and among learners?

(3) What has been your overall experience with social media as regards learning? In retrospect, can you pinpoint learning moments that arose while you were using and/ or communicating on the internet? Can you tease apart what made these moments 'instructional'?

Further reading

Balatti, J., Haase, M., Henderson, L. and Knight, C. (2010) Developing teacher professional identity through online learning: A social capital perspective. See https://researchonline.jcu.edu.au/16476/1/Professional_identity_Balatti_1-4-11.pdf (accessed 26 January 2018).

Coiro, J., Knobel, M., Lankshear, C. and Leu, D.J. (eds) (2014) *Handbook of Research on New Literacies*. London: Routledge.

Littlejohn, A., Beetham, H. and McGill, L. (2012) Learning at the digital frontier: A review of digital literacies in theory and practice. *Journal of Computer Assisted Learning* 28 (6), 547–556.

Meneses, J. and Mominó, J.M. (2010) Putting digital literacy in practice: How schools contribute to digital inclusion in the network society. *The Information Society* 26 (3), 197–208.

Mills, K.A. (2010) Shrek meets Vygotsky: Rethinking adolescents' multimodal literacy practices in schools. *Journal of Adolescent & Adult Literacy* 54 (1), 35–45.

Richardson, J.C. and Alsup, J. (2015) From the classroom to the keyboard: How seven teachers created their online teacher identities. *The International Review of Research in Open and Distributed Learning* 16 (1), 142–167.

Wilson, G. and Stacey, E. (2004) Online interaction impacts on learning: Teaching the teachers to teach online. *Australasian Journal of Educational Technology* 20 (1), 33–48.

References

Meskill, C. (2002) *Teaching and Learning in Real Time: Media, Technologies, and Language Acquisition*. Houston, TX: Athelstan.

Noddings, N. (2003) Is teaching a practice? *Journal of Philosophy of Education* 37 (2), 241–251.

Picciano, A.G., Seaman, J., Shea, P. and Swan, K. (2012) Examining the extent and nature of online learning in American K-12 education: The research initiatives of the Alfred P. Sloan Foundation. *The Internet and Higher Education* 15 (2), 127–135.

Stallard, C.K. and Cocker, J. (2014) *Education Technology and the Failure of American Schools*. Lanham, MD: Rowman & Littlefield.

Swingle, M. (2016) *i-Minds: How Cell Phones, Computers, Gaming, and Social Media are Changing Our Brains, Our Behavior, and the Evolution of Our Species.* Gabriola Island, BC: New Society.

Yukselturk, E. and Bulut, S. (2009) Gender differences in self-regulated online learning environment. *Journal of Educational Technology & Society* 12 (3), 12–22.

Glossary of terms

Academic discourse
Language particular to an academic subject or subjects.

Anchoring feedback
Facilitating discussion by periodically summarizing and pointing out key ideas, highlighting target concepts and providing examples and suggestions for consideration and further discussion.

Asynchronous environments
Venues where messages are posted and read at any time, not synchronously.

Attentiveness
The process whereby a learner focuses on material under study.

Blended learning
A course designed to take place partially face-to-face and partially online.

Blog
An asynchronous space for posting public writings on the internet.

Chat
Synchronous text-based communication.

CMC
Computer-mediated communication.

CMS
Course management system.

Collective feedback
A strategy involving both insiders and outsiders commenting and providing suggestions within course discussions.

Communication venue
The oral, written, synchronous or asynchronous mode for information exchange.

Comparative thinking
Applying and extending comparative and contrasting strategies to capture analogies and differences in order to generalize concepts.

Conversational approach
Teaching and learning via instructional conversations.

Corralling
Instructor (or a student) redirects learner's attention to specifics of language used and/or idea expressed.

Digital learning object
An online item specifically designed for instructional purposes.

Digital native
Learners born in the age of the internet.

Distance education
Teaching and learning via telecommunications.

Electronic portfolio
Cumulative, selected, annotated student work to demonstrate developing knowledge and competencies.

Explicit feedback
Direct correction of incorrect utterances.

Hybrid course
(see Blended) A course partially taught online and partially face-to-face.

Hyperlink
A link to a file or URL embedded within a text.

Implicit feedback
Indirect corrections of student mistakes often integrated into the flow of meaningful interactions.

Instructional conversation
A conversational move that contributes to learners' development in a particular area.

Instructional conversation strategy
A conversational method used to achieve a learning objective.

(Instructional) playfulness
Presenting complex academic matters in humorous and playful contexts by making material more comprehensive and engaging.

LMS
Learning management system. A suite of online tools used to develop an instructional environment.

MOOC
Massive open online course.

Multiparty conversation(s)/interaction(s)
Communication between and among many users of the same digital space.

Online corralling
A verbal means of cornering learners into thinking and communicating in discipline-appropriate ways in online activities, thereby demonstrating authentic mastery.

Online course
Typically used to describe a course that is 100% delivered via telecommunications.

Online instructional conversations
Conversations that are development directed, focused in ongoing assessment, student centered, with teachers structuring and guiding with an established focus in mind and concentrated on active use of new understandings in online contexts.

Online modeling
Producing models of the targeted content and skills throughout online activities.

Online saturating
Inundating instructional discourse with targeted vocabulary and accompanying conceptualizations.

Online teaching and learning
Teaching and learning using telecommunications.

Orchestrating interactions
Establishing and maintaining the topic and direction of communication intended for learning.

Peer feedback
Comments provided by students on each other's performance.

Podcast
Digital audio and video files available to play and download on the internet.

Providing feedback online
Responses to students in online activities that signal and direct learning.

Recasting
Reformulating an incorrect student utterance with the incorrect parts replaced with the corrected ones.

Scaffolding synthetic thinking
An instructional conversation strategy whereby both students and instructors scaffold one another's thinking and learning.

Synchronous environments
Venues for teaching and learning in real time.

Synthetic thinking
Learning by combining individual thoughts and ideas into a complex notion.

Task toolkit
The set of elements that make up the focus of a given assignment collected and managed in a course task repository and reused as needed. It typically has the form of a constant onscreen text box to which students can refer throughout as they type or record, review and revise their posts.

Teachable moment
Any segment of a lesson viewed by the lesson participants as an opportunity to develop further in a particular area.

Teaching in real time
Real-time text exchanges that can happen in written-only or oral/aural or combined modes.

Teaching with text
Teaching and learning via written asynchronous formats in the form of written text in discussion boards, blogs, emails or any other written asynchronous venue.

Teaching with voice
Teaching by posting and sharing multimodal messages consisting of sound via a telecommunications medium: emails, blogs, message boards, community messaging sites, etc.

Voicethreads
A recorded, asynchronous way of communication via the software http://voicethread.com/.

Index